WRITING THE QUALITATIVE DISSERTATION

Understanding by Doing

Second Edition

WRITING THE QUALITATIVE DISSERTATION

Understanding by Doing

Second Edition

Judith M. Meloy
Castleton State College

LEA LAWRENCE ERLBAUM ASSOCIATES, PUBLISHERS

2002   Mahwah, New Jersey   London

Lawrence Erlbaum Associates, Inc., Publishers
10 Industrial Avenue
Mahwah, NJ 07430

Cover design by Kathryn Houghtaling Lacey

Library of Congress Cataloging-in-Publication Data
   Meloy, Judith M.
   Writing the qualitative dissertation : understanding by doing ;
   Judith M. Meloy.—2nd ed.
   p. cm.
Includes bibliographical references and index.
   ISBN 0-8058-3288-2 (cloth : alk. paper) —
   ISBN 0-8058-3289-0 (pbk. : alk. paper)
   1. Dissertations, Academic—Authorship—Handbooks,
   manuals, etc. 2. Research—Methodology—Handbooks,
   manuals, etc. 3. Academic writing—Handbooks, manuals,
   etc. I. Title.

   LB2369 .M38 2001
   808'.02—dc21
                                                    00-067721
                                                         CIP

Books published by Lawrence Erlbaum Associates are printed
on acid-free paper, and their bindings are chosen for strength
and durability.

Printed in the United States of America
10 9 8 7 6 5 4 3 2 1

CONTENTS

RESEARCH CORRESPONDENTS

- Lew Allen, EdD (1992)
- Anonymous
- "Ann," doctoral student, first edition
- "Carol," EdD (1989)
- Dana Haight Cattani, PhD (1998)
- Mary K. Clark, PhD (1999)
- Pamela K. Edwards, PhD candidate (2000–2001)
- Robert M. Foster, EdD (1988)
- Katharine S. Furney, EdD (1997)
- Pat M. Garlikov, PhD (1990)
- Diana L. Haleman, EdD (1998)
- Linda S. Handelman, PhD (1995)
- Lisa A. Haston, doctoral student
- Kelly Clark Keefe, EdD (1999)
- Patricia Kovel-Jarboe, PhD (1986)

- Sharon Shockley Lee, EdD (1992)
- Timothy McCollum, graduate student, first edition
- Kimberly A. McCord, DME (1999)
- Sally Michlin, PhD (2000)
- Marie Wilson Nelson, EdD (1982)
- Kristin Park, PhD (1992)
- Jane F. Patton, EdD (1991)
- Paula Gastenveld Payne, EdD (1990)
- Maria Piantanida, PhD (1982)
- Susan L. Poch, PhD (1998)
- Gretchen S. Rauschenberg, PhD (1986)
- Barbara Smith Reddish, EdD (1999)
- Kathy Rojek, EdD (1991)
- Helen Rolfe, PhD (1990)
- Edwina Portelle Romero, PhD (1999)
- Janice Ross, PhD (1998)
- Kathryn A. Scherck, DNSc (1989)
- Stuart J. Sigman, PhD (1982)
- Jean M. Stevenson, PhD (1989)
- James Sullivan, EdD (1992)
- Marilyn Volger Urion, PhD (1998)
- Ellen Weber, PhD (1994)
- Glynn G. Wolar, PhD (1998)
- Christopher Worthman, PhD (1999)
- Nancy Zeller, PhD (1987)

FOREWORD

I was really pleased to see that you hope to include some more detailed letters in your book. What I find exciting about your research is that you'll include as much of *our* voice as possible—the voice and concerns of people doing or recently finished doing qualitative research.

—Ann, correspondent

The draft of your text has been extremely helpful to me at this juncture of my work. I come away from this reading with so many emotions—I can definitely see the value in correspondence and dialogue with others who have been through the maze.

—Carolyn Gabb, graduate student

I would love to have had your book while doing my dissertation.

—Kathryn Scherck,
DNSc, RN, correspondent

ACKNOWLEDGMENTS

I would like to thank the publisher and my editor, Naomi Silverman. Without her encouragement, patience, care, and insight, I would not have completed this second edition. As Egon Guba used to tell me, "Judy, things take longer than they do." Naomi, thank you. In addition, several professors helped connect with many of the correspondents for this second edition. Thanks especially to: Donna Alverman, Maenette Benham, Elliot Eisner, Corinne Glesne, Larry Lesser, and Chris Pappas, among others. It also goes without saying that those who enabled the first edition remain the foundation of this one, including the correspondents and my mom and dad. This time, however, I also wish to acknowledge the children of my brother and sisters (John, Beth, and Lydia), because the two oldest, John and Matt, brought out the book to show off to their friends after Matt's rehearsal dinner party! Who would have thought this book to be prenuptial entertainment? Indeed, all of my siblings' children—Jan, Jeff, Mark, Charlie, Christopher, Ali, Lydia, and Jacque make me proud to be a teacher and learner. Finally, I must repeat myself. I remain sincerely beholden to the correspondents of both editions, without whose generosity this work would not exist.

ABOUT THIS BOOK

One of the most common ways we have of learning to do something is by doing it. But unlike fastening our shoes or baking a cake—processes that have been simplified by the introduction of Velcro and "just add oil" mixes—'doing' research is becoming more complex and controversial. Although qualitative researchers are making substantial contributions to scholarship by describing not only how research is conceptualized but also how its products are finally presented and understood, there is, for novice researchers and traditionally trained faculty members across the wide array of disciplines, a down side. As the number of methodological options and alternative presentations of research increase, so does the ambiguity for those who will be answering questions such as:

- Which paradigm, methodology, or methods do I use?
- What are the particular standards (philosophical, practical) for doing qualitative research?
- What exactly is meant by "qualitative research"?
- What is the basis for the analysis and interpretation of experience?
- How does any chosen ideological stance or methodological framework enable justifiable, rigorous research?

- What will the representation/presentation of the research look like?

At the beginning of the 21st century, it is still the case that not all interested inquirers are getting direct, in-depth support for learning about and doing qualitative research. Many books have been written, stemming from Lincoln and Guba's (1985) classic, *Naturalistic Inquiry*, to the second edition of Glesne's (1999) *Becoming Qualitative Researchers*. In contrast to texts that provide instruction on "how" to do qualitative research, **the purpose of this book is to share, in rich detail, understandings of how it <u>feels</u> and what it <u>means</u> to do qualitative research for the doctoral dissertation**. In this second edition, correspondents continue to write freely about their emotional journeys, their explicit concern with ethical issues, and the "so what?" nature of research. They share with their cohort from the first edition their excitement and reasoning behind their decision making; many laud their mentors and institutions of higher education for the challenge, support, and freedom to take the risks that contemplating, doing, and representing qualitative research require.

Why This Book?

Initially, I drafted this book in response to my doctoral dissertation research experience. I emerged from those months during the spring of 1986 with a set of reoccurring questions, concerns, feelings, and needs that had not gone away. I was sure others choosing to use qualitative methodologies were also going through similar periods of doubt and euphoria. I was sure guidelines existed somewhere—that is, someone had already interpreted for the novice what it meant to work through an emergent design from proposal to final defense; someone had thought about what it meant—as a student and human being—to be the research "instrument" of choice. I was sure <u>somebody</u> could describe how the form of a qualitative dissertation—from the statement of the problem through the presentation of the data and the analysis and interpretation of results—differed from a traditional five chapter, third person thesis. But I was unable to find "the" exemplar to help me. What I did find were several examples of 'qualitative' theses that had been written and successfully defended at Indiana University before mine. What seemed clear, however, after working through the experience for myself, was that the overall format and internal structure of qualitative dissertations were different from those that had come before.

A catalyst for completing a second edition of this book has been my continued professional life since 1986. I have listened to the stories of graduate students and faculty members who, alone and cooperatively, have been working through what it means to do qualitative research. I have heard questions, confusions, answers, interpretations, joys, and sorrows. I continue to see how eagerly graduate students want to share and get support for what they are trying to figure out and accomplish. I have heard faculty members seeking fuller understanding so that they can interact positively with their students, because it is not, as one correspondent writes, "as easy as it looks." Both enthusiastic e-mails and snail mail from readers of the first edition not only convince me that the correspondents and I have "done good," as my Aunt Jean would say with a smile, but also reinforce the potential value of a second edition.

I remain convinced that explicating the simultaneous and multifaceted processes of inquiry, that is, the conscious and tacit learning–thinking–researching–feeling–interpreting–knowing–writing, ensures our ability to do qualitative research better. The complexity of the researcher as the human instrument has only begun to be explicated. Indeed, that is why I separated the actions in the previous sentence with hyphens instead of commas; the workings are connected and multiple rather than discrete and linear. They imply more than one level of processing at a time.

Doing qualitative research for one's thesis requires a conscious, internal awareness within the external structural, political, and human context of higher education because the dissertation is the focus of intense personal interaction and ambiguity around such tasks as forming a dissertation committee or choosing an area of interest. The correspondents, whose reflections are the data source for this book, <u>describe some of the interactions and sources of ambiguity that are a part of the process of qualitative research</u> and hence of concern to doctoral students choosing qualitative research methodologies for their thesis research.

About the Study and the Second Edition

Both editions of this book are the result of making contact with individuals who are working on or have completed qualitative dissertations. *The Chronicle of Higher Education* provided room for a brief advertisement in the spring of 1990 and in the fall of 1998 and 1999. In 1998, colleagues whose doctoral students were working on or completing qualitative dissertations suggested potential correspondents as well.

For the first edition, I focused mainly on the issues of structure and format; I asked specific questions of the correspondents, such as Did you use first or third person in your thesis? How many chapters did you have? Why? What resources were invaluable to you? What assumptions did you make? Did you keep a journal? I asked interested individuals to write me a letter pertaining to these or any other decision rules they made that resulted in the final form of their theses. For the second edition, the focusing questions changed dramatically to include: Did you use an action, feminist, critical, collaborative, or arts-based approach? Is collaboration an important topic for you? Technology? What issues emerged during analysis and interpretation? Were emotional or ethical issues salient to you? Finally, I asked all correspondents to include references that supported their work and to write about anything else that entered their minds. Fortunately, for us, they did.

Audience

The target audience for this book is and always has been doctoral students. I think those of us who have gone through the experience have something to offer those who will choose to do so. I believe that a book offering a variety of perspectives on what it means and feels like to do qualitative research for the doctoral dissertation provides an alternative conception of support not unlike Ely's (1991) *Doing Qualitative Research: Circles Within Circles.* In addition, upon reading this book, faculty members, friends, and family of qualitative researchers can better appreciate the absorbing *milieu* facing novice qualitative researchers.

Each individual reader will bring his/her own experiences and expectations to this book. At one level, the material may be regarded as a compilation of "war stories," the thick description and recollection of a particular experience from a variety of perspectives. The question of "so what?" is answered by acknowledging that we do learn vicariously from other people's experience; we also feel about their experiences and learn from those feelings. Our cognition and feelings combine in ways that enable us as individuals to regard our contemporary experiencing from a variety of perspectives, and hence judge it, hone it, foster it, or reshape it. Depending on who you are, certain episodes will mean more than others, certain caveats or suggestions will seem more salient. Nevertheless, this book may focus, enable, or guide both doctoral students and dissertation committee members in their conversations around qualitative research issues (Morgan, 1983). Finally, although I do not interpret my role as qualitative researcher and writer to be that of a judge ruling on the experiences of my correspondents, I do have several concerns that I indicate as they appear throughout the book. I hope that some of the issues raised encourage the continuation of the concerned dialogue about the qualities and quality of qualitative research.

Structure and Style

Structure. The organization of the chapters emerged from my interest in providing support for the processes of qualitative research. The processes are foundational to the whole of the research experience, although understanding that whole rarely happens until the end of a work. Therefore, I chose to begin this book with a chapter about "the end," where an amount of certainty and confidence finally emerges for the novice qualitative researcher. In addition, I pose a set of "QUESTIONS" in each chapter that became explicit as a result of my interaction with the correspondents' ideas. These questions extend beyond the original focusing ones of this study and can be considered a part of my analysis process. The questions are, in a strict sense, neither solved nor answered. I will disappoint all readers looking for the "right" answers. I also do not presume the questions are unique or original. However, I do intend, by asking them here, to locate the questions in one place in explicit, written form. I believe these questions will prod you to consider the totality of the research endeavor as you encounter seemingly discrete concerns.

I also chose, finally, to use headings to provide additional focus points. I believe the headings themselves are arbitrary; the themes of the letters run into each other throughout this book. Other points in the letters offer additional concerns. However, because headings can serve to reduce initial ambiguity, I believe they may be of some value here. I have also created a detailed index of major and minor themes.

Style. My predisposition in this volume is to be informal. I have had many one-on-one conversations with doctoral students and faculty members; "you" has always been the form of address, that is, "What are you thinking?" or "How are you managing?" I will try not to be too comfortable with you, the reader, but I do not want a formal tone to block the personal and personable nature of this research. The data are letters; my correspondents and I came to know each other through both snail mail and e-mail. Together we are thinking and sharing out loud. I want them to speak to you in the same way.

In most cases, I use the correspondents' first names with their contributions; whenever I thought the material might be harmful, I deleted any attribution. We went back and forth about this; I have permissions from all of them. My correspondents stand by their reflections; my final decision, however, has been to provide anonymity around certain issues in order to enable the issue to take precedence over where and with whom it occurred. In addition, each correspondent had the opportunity to edit the excerpts and letters I have included in this book. I was more cautious than they were; I remain responsible for any errors in judgment.

In order to provide a sense of the research context as I experienced it, I include some lengthy excerpts from the correspondents' letters containing more than one point. I have tried not to select out "the" point I think the correspondents are making. I have also tried not to reduce their contributions to the particular sense I want to make. I do clarify the points I use to connect the experiences of the correspondents together; I hope this will not stop you from finding different points of interest or debate, or a different sense of the whole. I believe this book will enable all of us to become more consciously aware of the complexity surrounding the issues and possible nuances of our decision making. If, together, the correspondents and I have accomplished presenting a range of experiences for your consideration, then I believe this book will become your volume of conclusions and sense rather than ours. The book is meant as a means rather than an end, as an offering rather than an imperative. Marilyn shares this sense of offering with the opening to her dissertation. Because her research is about writing dissertations, incorporating her thoughts here feels most appropriate.

Offering

At [almost] fifty

one of the problems

with going back to school for a Ph.D.

is that it's hard to think

of doing a dissertation

just to be done with it—just to get on with my life.

At fifty [almost]

I am already into my life

and my hours are too few to spend without passion.

And at [almost] fifty

I am tired of whittling my voice to fit incongruous spaces

and impatient with softening the edges of what I say.

At [almost] fifty

I am [almost] willing to risk revolution—

I am well into my life

and my words are too many to write without passion.

And my words, at fifty, are expansive—

I breathe in and the scent of stars swirls with mockorange.

I reach to pick up a cone dropped by a great white pine

and the tips of my fingers meet the cold at the edge
of the universe.

I bite into the firm, green skin of a ripened pear

and my tongue recoils at the sharp grit of a falling star.

I sit with my fingers on the keyboard

and words from a thousand generations clamor to be
spoken.

At fifty I am willing to risk metamorphosis

and my hours are too few to spend without play.

At [just past] fifty I give you my words.

They are without boundaries

the scent of ripe pears and mockorange

the cold of hyperspace,

the sharp grit of falling stars,

words of a thousand generations' passion and play clamoring

at the edge of the universe—

revolution

for your pleasure.

In a critique of an earlier draft of some of this material, an anonymous reviewer stated: "I really don't see much of a point to all of this except, perhaps, to make the qualitative researcher 'feel good.'" Such an objective remains a fundamentally humane and worthy purpose for this book. I welcome your comments and concerns. Write to: Judith Meloy, Poultney, VT 05764.

1

UNDERSTANDING
BY FINISHING

The End Is the Beginning

> Remember that conducting and writing up qualitative research is an evolutionary and inductive process. It's not a predictable or finite event; rather, it needs time and space to grow and change. (Katie)

Although I was never alone in my graduate research classes, I found I was always alone as I was collecting and analyzing data for my thesis. I did not have the companionship of an a priori hypothesis or a statistical design to guide and structure me. None of my courses had required the intense interaction between doing and thinking on such sustained and multiple levels. With the general focus of my dissertation taped on the wall in front of my desk, I continuously had to attend to the tangents of analysis, letting them play themselves out in order to understand which paths, if any, were worth pursuing, or whether the emerging foci or indeed the general one with which I began needed adjusting. I was alone with notes all over the place—organized chaos—and yet never alone, as there were always thoughts sprouting in a brain partially numbed to anything but them. I had no idea what "doing all of this" meant, and, at times, I wondered whether I could do it at all. It was like struggling with a team of wild horses pulling a runaway wagon.

Because the efforts to understand and manage my thesis research are as memorable as the substance of the thesis itself, I am convinced that neither course work and texts about how to understand and do qualitative research nor the beginnings of my own efforts to learn by doing would be the appropriate starting point for a book about the <u>experiencing</u> of such things. Those of us who have completed at least one major research project using qualitative methodologies have learned it is only AT THE END of the experience that we begin to see the whole we constructed. For some committees and current graduate students such "last minute" knowing is not yet acceptable—"What are the a priori foci?" and "What will you have when you are finished?" are examples of questions we have been led to believe we should be able to answer from the very beginning.

BY THE END of the dissertation experience I was able to explain why the thesis looked like it did. At the beginning, I did not understand the concept of "being able to handle ambiguity" in any practical way. I had a sense of the practicalities of working with a committee of four different individuals but did not actually know what to expect. At the beginning, I did not know how different from my ordinary ways of making sense of the world the dissertation research process was going to be. In spite of my course work, I had no idea what it felt like to do research. Writing the dissertation was an experience in itself; adding qualitative research on top of that made for an especially interesting time of learning, reflection, and practice. I often felt like I was playing a game of pickup sticks while balancing on a high wire over an empty river in the middle of a moonless night. What qualitative researchers learn AT THE END is that ambiguity is a puzzlement that is resolved through learning-by-doing. The high wire of not knowing does come to ground, and, most often, it does so safely.

What does a qualitative dissertation look like at THE END? I believe a sense of the answer to that question can be found in two letters from recent correspondents whose descriptions of experience foreshadow both old and new themes that the remaining chapters of this book explicate. Susan's letter provides the opening to many of the themes discussed in the following chapters. A second lengthy letter, which concludes chapter 10, pulls many themes together again.

> Hi Judy, My name is Susan Poch and I just recently finished my dissertation and successfully defended it (April 1998). I don't know if that makes me a statistic or just what, but I did finish! [(9/21/00)]

> [(10/8/98)] I began my doctoral degree by default. My husband is employed in the area and we have children, 5 to be exact, who were and are attending school here. It was impossible to think of going anywhere else. But fortunately, my department hired an exceptional faculty member who

accepted me as her student. She helped me through the prelim process, and I'm not sure that at that point she was sure of my capabilities. But we managed to develop a good working relationship (which I believe is absolutely essential in a chair–student situation!) and pressed on....

Students are taught about qualitative research in my department from an ethnographical viewpoint. We are told that we should develop an interest or a "what's going on here" perspective, immerse ourselves in the situation, gather all the data possible (interviews, documents, observations), and analyze the data with some framework that would emerge from the data. Then and only then would a literature review be attempted—essentially, working backward from the data to the introduction is the proper technique. However, when my chair and I talked about a proposal, she told me that I would have a literature review and a theoretical framework in my proposal, *even before I knew what I was going to find*. How could this be done? The three proposals I used for examples and help (two of which had been successfully defended) contained neither of these things. But being a dutiful student who believes the chair knows best, I did what I was told.

I am eternally grateful for the path my chair laid out for me. Because of her insistence, I was able to use the literature review, methodological chapter, and introduction from my proposal, in my dissertation. What a life/time saver! While it was difficult in my proposal to try to guess what I might find in my data, it still gave me a framework for questions and a path to follow.

My chair is from a policy background, so my study was policy oriented. My study started out being about transfer students' perceptions of their time-to-degree at 4-year institutions. I decided to use focus groups as my primary form of data collection because the students had a common experience (transfer), and I wanted to get a great deal of data in a short amount of time. (Don't we all? ☺) As I was moving along on this path, it became increasingly apparent that there was a state-mandated policy that had been handed down to these institutions regarding accountability, more specifically, efficient graduation. No one had ever touched on how transfer students impact these mandates, nor had anyone ever asked transfer students how the mandates impacted them. So, the focus shifted from just transfer students and their experiences to the policy and administrators at these institutions and their perceptions of transfer students and the mandates. Twelve administrators, 42 transfer students, and 3 site visits later, I was faced with a mound of data that was only slightly relevant to my proposal.

In the meantime, of course, my chair told me that I would need to take an additional class. (I had already finished my program.) She said, "you are going to be doing the work anyway, so you might as well sign up for credit and not just audit it." Great. This was fall semester 1997; I wanted to defend my proposal, get all of my data collected by Christmas, and be doing analysis over Christmas break. It was impossible to do a class, too! But, again, I did what I was told. (Perhaps I should say here that I am 41 years old, I have children, and I've been around the block at least once. I am not just somebody who rolls over without question. However, I also believe that your chair should ultimately be respected, and you should just do what you're supposed to do. If you have a decent chair, that respect will be reciprocated, and you'll really come out ahead.)

The class was, of course, a policy class. Because I really didn't have any background in policy and was attempting a policy study for a dissertation, it was probably sound advice from my chair. Indeed, it turned out to be a very good way to develop pieces of the policy that would wind up as a chapter in my dissertation. She is so sly!

I did defend my proposal in early September (I had the luxury of devoting my summer to writing it.) Once my committee gave me their blessing, I was ready to roll. But the snag was that while I had communicated with the three institutions about when and what I wanted to do, there was a BIG lag time in when I was ready and when they could schedule me, or for that matter, even respond to my requests. That was the first major hurdle in my data collection. Patience is not easy when you see the days, weeks, months pass without much progress being made writing. Of course, my chair suggested that I could start preliminary analysis before all of the data were collected. Of course I could. Get real. How was I supposed to do that? It turned out that I collected data at two of the institutions by December and the third in January.

The paper requirements were finished for the policy class, I had collected all of my data, I had virtually three chapters all ready to plug in to the dissertation. Now what was the hold up? Where should I start? I sat for nearly 2 weeks wondering what to do next. I really couldn't afford too much of that because I had set a goal for myself. I wanted to walk through ceremonies in early May, which meant that I had to be finished and defended by the middle of April. It was nearing February.

What followed was a remarkable series of events at which I still marvel. I had (have) three friends who listened, helped me focus, and encouraged me endlessly through the process. The original model in the proposal simply would not work now, so one friend made me talk out all of my data so that she could understand what I saw and heard. Then she made me talk out how I visualized it all fitting together. She pushed me to think! I wound up reorganizing my chapters to a more logical flow and using a theoretical framework that I knew about but hadn't considered. The second friend simply said, "Just start." He encouraged me to take the

three chapters from my proposal and put them in the correct
format. Just keep at it. No excuses, just start. He wouldn't
hear anything else. The third friend, my neighbor, walked
with me every night. She helped with my physical health.
Couple that with the fact that I had an office (away from
home) where I could shut the door and concentrate; no
classes to take, none to teach, nothing but writing. Plus, my
chair knew when I was working or socializing. Drat!

I gave her a first draft (7 of 8 chapters) the second week of
March. I had successfully written the bulk of my dissertation in 6 weeks. Then I took a week off for Spring Break
and tended to my Golden Retriever, who had nine puppies
that week. Great timing, don't you think? In fact, I believe
that because I had children, puppies, a household, and a
husband, I both cherished my writing time (because it was
limited) and savored the real life that was happening
around me. The real life kept me sane during the writing. I
wouldn't recommend this method to everyone, but it was
really my only option.

The rest of the remarkable events include the fact that my
chair gave me back the first draft virtually free from any editorial comments. She was really a bit surprised about what
I had given her. She prides herself on being a good
writer—just ask her, she'll tell you. So, even though she expected good work from me (she really does have great faith
in me) she didn't expect it to be as good as it was. Whew!
You have no idea how that improved my self-esteem. I
wanted it to be good, but I was really scared. I had revised
my proposal five times, after all. I finished the final chapter
in about a week, revised the whole shebang a couple of
times, and left for a conference. Can you believe this? I had
to defend a week after I returned from the conference and I
was totally prepared! I had done all the paperwork, submitted it to all the committee members, written abstracts, and

had the format blessing from the graduate school. You cannot say that I didn't have someone looking out for me! The defense was successful; I was overjoyed, and I left the building that day saying, "My work here is done."

Themes emerging from Susan's letter include student–faculty relationships, the role of the chair, the importance and placement of the literature review, gaining entry, patience, "snags," support, and fear. Of the potential a priori themes the correspondents for the second edition could address (see About This Book), the one of especial importance to this group is the autobiographical nature of qualitative research. In addition, these writers concur with several correspondents from the first edition in their desire to do original research. The resulting emotional "teeter totter," not only of such a choice but also of the total qualitative research experience, remains a strong theme. Additional themes shared across editions include the cost and size of a qualitative dissertation; the writing of the proposal and the final product; and issues of ethics, power, and control. The use of technology to support research is made most explicit in the closing letter (chap. 10), and the work, continuity, and completion of this book were vastly facilitated by it as well. Within the discussions of voice, ownership, autobiography, and writing, themes of positionality and forms of representation appear.

2

UNDERSTANDING
BY BEGINNING

What Does a Qualitative
Dissertation Look Like?

The "finished product" looks very much like a "traditional"
dissertation, although it is much longer than most.… It appears in one HEAVY volume. It is not something you'd
want to fall on your foot. (Jean)

At the beginning of the 21st century, qualitative research is more widely accepted in graduate schools than ever before. However, several correspondents let me know that acceptance is more likely in schools of education
than elsewhere. One correspondent writes:

Although I *should have* gotten my PhD in ———, I was
advised early on in my graduate study that I would have a
much easier time doing a dissertation in the education department, especially since I already had a vision of what I
wanted to write about. I took this advice, although I took
many courses in my discipline and got an MA in it.…
Compared with many of my fellow students, I had a relatively easy time of getting a very alternative dissertation
approved and completed.

A second correspondent concurs: "My doctorate is truly politically moti-
vated, and, contrary to the wishes of my department Chair, it will be in education, but the subject matter is in my discipline." A third correspondent
describes interviewing for a position in her discipline after successfully de-

fending her thesis. (Yes, qualitative researchers do defend successfully and find employment!) This individual's experience suggests that qualitative researchers still have obstacles to face:

> I recently interviewed at a major research University where one of the old guard was filling in for a semester. He sat in on my talk-through of a syllabus for a qualitative research course in our discipline. When I described how I had been questioning when research questions should be written (realizing that they should be written after the researcher had spent some time at the site collecting data), he called me a radical and got up and left!

These former doctoral students made choices, and they all found their way; none of them describe a horrific or totally negative dissertation experience. In fact, the majority of the correspondents in both editions share their enthusiasm about the experience. Some of that enthusiasm is post hoc, some is ongoing. Knowing where you can learn about qualitative research, knowing where you will find institutions, departments, professors, and colleagues to support your learning and decision making will be essential to your success. Lisa knows exactly why she returned to school: "I had for a long time felt that my decision to stay home and rear my sons was a decision that was not highly regarded … as a valid one. I needed to prove … that I was intelligent, industrious, and worthy."

QUESTIONS

1. Why did you choose to earn a doctorate? Do your reasons influence your choice of study, methodology, and commitment?
2. How did you select your university? Did you know what you wanted to do and with whom you wanted to work? Will the choices you have made support your dissertation research endeavor?
3. Is your department or discipline supportive of qualitative research? Is your university? Do you know where qualitative expertise can be found on your campus?

One way many novice qualitative researchers want to learn about qualitative research is by examining model proposals or reviewing successfully defended qualitative dissertations. At the same time, many correspondents come to conclude that the "right" one doesn't exist for them. Reading about how qualitative dissertations appear and "hearing" the correspondents' reasoning around issues of form and structure may help you think through the possibilities and constraints imposed by this type of research.

FORMAT OPTIONS

Process Influences

For the first edition, I asked the correspondents about the number of chapters in their dissertation. The nuance I found interesting in the two passages that follow is the manner in which both Pat and Carol expressed their answers. Pat writes: "I ended up with 7 chapters. I followed a nontraditional, 7 chapter approach including a final summary. My appendices include the transcribed episodes, content analysis by line, along with the usual forms for permission and pictures." Carol uses the same language and implies that the number of chapters was the result of, not the predestination for, the substance of her thesis. She, too, *ended up with* [italics added] seven chapters. They are, in order, (1) the introduction, (2) the review of the literature, (3) the methodology, (4) the emerging themes essential to the process …, (5) an educative inquiry …, (6) a constitutive response …, and (7) the concluding implications."

I interpret the phrase "ending up" with any number of chapters to imply that the form originated from the nature of the research study itself, that is, from the interaction of the researcher with the context and with the analysis and interpretation of that context. This notion is congruent with the concept of emergent design so critical to qualitative research. Whether Pat and Carol knew it explicitly, they describe the final form of their theses as a result of their efforts and not as an a priori structure they followed in order to document and legitimate their studies. An anonymous correspondent describes the formulation of the thesis format as follows:

> The contents [of my thesis] are organized according to principles of Chinese cosmology and numerology: 3 parts, a focus on chapter 5, 9 chapters, and so on. The organization sort of emerged appropriate to the content. My disser-

tation integrates materials from several disciplines, including geography, anthropology, folklore, history, botany, philosophy, and others; to comprehend the central idea, one has to peel it like an onion.... Similarly, my conceptual framework (perhaps a house made of sticks) seemed "natural to me." I didn't attempt to get the "right answers" and may have speculated too much. My conclusion was really a handful of suggestions resulting from a mass of interrelated observations and insights I gained during the research process. Overall, writing the dissertation was a pleasant experience.

Nancy suggests that both personal background and graduate course work in qualitative research influenced the development of her thesis structure:

My dissertation has 6 chapters. I followed no format or guidelines beyond the useful suggestions of two key faculty members. I would guess that my dissertation is "traditional" when compared with those in the humanities and the more qualitatively oriented social sciences (e.g., cultural anthropology), but nontraditional when compared with dissertations in education and the more quantitatively oriented social sciences (e.g., psychology).... I would guess that my background ... had a lot to do with how my dissertation project was conceived and carried out. I purposely did not look at any other dissertations before writing mine because I wanted mine to be original and, more importantly, to embody a form that was congruent with naturalistic inquiry.

Qualitative researchers seem to develop a sense of a study's coherence, which is dictated by the project itself rather than any suggested a priori plan or structure. However, Maria had an a priori goal. She writes:

In my own case, I wanted to submit my dissertation for publication as a book that would be read by practitioners who would have little understanding of or patience for reading a research rationale. Therefore, I put my discussion of research methods in chapter 4. Chapter 3 contained the substantive theory of practice that I had generated from my study. Chapter 5 contained a formal theory of professional practice that I generated as a result of my reflections on the research process and myself as an evolving scholar. One of my committee members argued during my defense that a dissertation is a dissertation, not a book. We went back and forth about this, but in the end, we agreed to disagree and the format remained unchanged.

Janice makes the following observation:

> One of the dictums of art is that "form follows function"; for the qualitative dissertation writer this can be profoundly true as well. It seems to me that there are dissertation topics that beg for qualitative research.... Their content or "function," asks for a qualitative "form."

Tradition's Influence

Other correspondents talked differently about what made sense to them. Kathryn asserts that a traditional research format—Introduction/Problem, Literature Review, Methodology/Procedures, Analysis, Conclusions—was appropriate for her study.

> Why does my dissertation look the way it does? First off, yes, Kerlinger would recognize it. There are the typical five chapters. This was not dictated by my committee or any house rules. No other form made sense. I tried doing a more qualitative format but discarded it because it did not leave a sufficient "paper trail" for anyone else to follow. Granted, it was initially hard to separate what needed to go into the Results chapter and what needed to go into Discussion. The rule I developed was level of abstraction: That which appeared as cold, clinical description (how many said what) went into the Results section; that which was more story-like was included in the Dis-

cussion section. To reduce the boredom of qualitative data presented in this way and enhance believability, I used a lot of examples and quotes in Results, which was a lengthy chapter. My three quantitative committee members did not challenge it in any way. In addition, I had quantitative data as well as qualitative. It did not make sense to do it any other way. I did not want to lose the sense of how interrelated were the two types of data. Although each type of datum was derived from a different research question, the study would have been less meaningful if separated.

Several other correspondents write that their theses retained a traditional chapter structure as well. Patricia's dissertation "is formatted along traditional lines with five chapters and appendices." Robert's also has five chapters: "I was influenced by traditional designs, but the presentation is unique. Chapter 4 presents the context in a lengthy narrative describing and capturing (I hope) the daily goings on at the site." [NOTE: You can find more information about each of the correspondents Appendix A. In addition, several correspondents have volunteered their Tables of Contents, which you can find in Appendix B.]

Across these descriptions, qualitative researchers reveal themselves to be conscious, interactive sensemakers—that is, what makes sense to one may not be an exemplar for another. The choices and subsequent decisions made are grounded in the individual's perception of his or her focus and overall research purposes, that is, what will work "for me." Perhaps the observable structure or format of the qualitative dissertation—including the number of chapters, headings, inclusion and type of data, appendixes, audit trails, and so forth—provides readers with explicit clues to the researcher's processes of analysis and interpretation, which are a part of the meaning of the study. If this idea makes sense, then the notion of an "appropriate" format for qualitative dissertations probably does not exist unless it is explicitly linked to the substance and context of the study and the methodology that generated it. Marie, a correspondent in the first edition, comments on the emerging design of her thesis as well as her study.

The chapter titles show how I drew on tradition and circumvented it:

Chapter I.   Definition of the Problem

Chapter II.   A Context for Inquiry (literature review)

> Like my study, my dissertation had an emergent design, and this was no accident. My goal was not to present reductive abstractions about what I had learned. It was to help others learn, to guide readers—my participants and other researchers—through the learning-research processes I had gone through.

As Marie suggests, the presentation of her study required a format compatible with it. I must have believed this in the spring of 1986, when I wrote the Foreword of my thesis:

> Dear Reader:
>
> More and more dissertations that might be described as "naturalistic" or "qualitative" are being completed. This dissertation is an example of a naturalistic study in which qualitative methods were used. This terminology will be explained in chapter I. However, I would first like to give you a preview of what to expect, as the format and style of this dissertation may be different from others you have read. (Meloy, 1986)

I am not trying to suggest I was right all along. However, my continued participation in the world of qualitative research since the defense of my thesis leads me to conclude that the congruence of what we do <u>and</u> how we present it (the result of our implicit sense of the study's "whole") is as important to qualitative studies as are the explicit structures that define and allow us to examine an experimental study. Does the format we choose somehow exemplify—rather than predetermine—the study? I think so. Dana suggests how times are changing:

When I finished collecting data, I met with each committee member to discuss the dissertation format. Without exception, they emphasized that I should write something *interesting*. When I proposed to them a very traditional outline of chapters (Introduction, Literature Review, Methodology, Data Chapters, etc.), they encouraged me to reconceive the design. My notes from our conversations include the following advice: Be literary. Write for yourself. Cite nothing that isn't directly relevant. Put everything else (literature review and methodology) in an annotated appendix. Maintain a sense of movement and direction. Assume an intellectual—but not academic—view. Think *Crown Books*. Write an academically respectable document that is also a page-turner. Anything you say should be justified either by your data or existing literature or both. Write theme chapters (not data chapters). Use metaphor and analogy. Write a snappy introduction.

… The overwhelming sense I got from my committee members was that the unpardonable sin was to be boring.

I felt incredibly liberated by their advice and unfettered as a writer. That is not to say that the writing was easy. It wasn't. However, I was sustained by my committee's obvious commitment to substantive, readable research.

Dana hints at possibilities for divergent, alternative formats and dissertation presentations, yet correspondents for the second edition did not describe in much detail their thesis defenses or emphasize the "alternative" nature of their work. [See Katie's description of her writing, chap. 7, pp.119–122, for an exception to this statement.] In a way, this makes sense. For newcomers who are learning how to think and do differently, a traditional research format offers the comfort (and burden) of a set of assumptions about how to present the material in order that it might be more easily comprehended. As several correspondents across the years have written, "I needed to get this thing done." Alternative dissertation presentations, on the other hand, require a significant level of attention from both the researcher and his or her audience. Until recently, readers of research have not had to struggle with the material on a variety of levels except, perhaps, with some statistical terminology in order to grasp "the" point. The implicit nature of the "objective" research report led us to expect "good" research to be presented that way. A characteristic of contemporary qualitative research, offered by experienced researchers and attempted by novice ones, are formats and representations that eschew univocal, linear text (e.g., Cole & Knowles, 2000); structures, formats and presentations of qualitative research are polyvocal, collaborative, and complex. They can appear to complicate while they simultaneously clarify the multiple processes of learning, reflecting, analyzing, interpreting, and portraying that qualitative research is. For example, "troubling" texts demand more from their readers (e.g., Cruz, 2000; Lather, 1991) than qualitative dissertations recently defended. How far the neophyte qualitative researcher wishes to extend his or her experimenting while completing a qualitative dissertation will depend greatly on both institutional and personal factors yet to be described. The concept of risk in choosing and doing such research appears throughout this text.

For some correspondents, the structure and format of the dissertation held no risk. Although those cited so far appear to have had a great deal of say about the final format of their thesis, others did not. Jean relates:

> I had to use the University's (Graduate School's) approved format: chapter 1—Introduction; chapter 2—Review of the Literature; chapter 3—Methodology; chapters 4 and 5—"The Body"; and chapter 6—Conclusions (in my case Reflections and Implications). There was some pressure (which I resisted) to provide my committee with the first three chapters before they would consider accepting my study.

> The "finished product" ... is 406 pages—with 316 pages of actual text. There are seven separate appendixes contributing 51 pages. I resisted the Graduate School's insistence that it should appear in two volumes, because I did not want it separated in any way for fear that continuity would be lost. My committee agreed with me.

Although Jean seems to emphasize the size of her dissertation, at least two other issues are salient here. The first is that Jean argues for the *continuity* of her work, which I interpret to be compatible with the concept of the "whole" under discussion. The second issue of interest to me is the presentation of the role of the graduate school in shaping her dissertation decisions. The freedom—or lack thereof—of doctoral students to make decisions about their work has grabbed my attention. I wonder how often this next story remains the case?

> Can I be facetious? My dissertation looks like this because that's the way my major professor wanted it to look. My advisor had the "power"; I was <u>only</u> a <u>VIP</u> (very important peon) student, and I wanted to complete the thesis in a timely fashion. Seriously, all decision rules were reasonable decisions to which I had little trouble adhering.

> The final form of my dissertation is traditional, with one exception; it has 6 chapters instead of 5. I did a pilot study in order to sharpen my research skill. My <u>committee</u> wanted me to include the pilot study in the dissertation, although I did not use the findings for the final summary and conclusions. I agreed, but stated to my major advisor that I wanted it to be in a separate chapter, to avoid confusing the reader. That was okay.

Gretchen suggests another reason why freedom of choice may be limited: "The general rule was that the format of the dissertation would be 'traditional'; justification was the potential for publication in academic journals. I accepted this with no problem, because I hoped for publication as soon as possible."

SUMMARY

It seems, then, that qualitative dissertations look like they do for reasons that <u>may</u> be integrally connected to the type of research undertaken. Factors such as institutional expectations, individual assertiveness and risk taking, timeliness, and hopes for professional publication may mitigate against an emergent, nontraditional format and structure. Kathy, who introduced my presentation at the Qualitative Research in Education conference sponsored by the School of Education at the University of Georgia in 1989, writes about several of these concerns as well:

> When I returned home after your session at the Qualitative Research Conference, I wished I had gone home before lunch and not returned. I found the experience very unsettling. Many of the concerns and frustrations expressed were concerns of graduate students doing any type of dissertation.... I regretted not making a comment about the uncertainty involved for both graduate students and major professors in working through a qualitative study. I think the uncertainty is as agonizing for major professors who care about research, their reputations, and their students. Each study is different and the questions that emerge need to be dealt with. It was argued that models do exist. They may not exist in all academic departments at all universities and colleges. And if they do exist not all of us are aware of what the models are. I have looked at a number of dissertations. My advisor has, too. There are things each of us like about certain parts of each of the dissertations we have screened. Other dissertations have presented possibilities. None of them has served as a model for the case study I am writing.

By outward appearances, some dissertations using qualitative research methodologies look like traditional, quantitative theses. We are still in the process of identifying ways of communicating exemplary qualitative research. We have been focusing on how to do the research well, which is important for both novice and experienced researchers. That we present it in a manner that honors the process while evoking understanding is also important. For novices, the latter emphasis may suggest additional difficulties, because aspects of the qualitative research process are inexorably intuitive and implicit—internal and integral to the human being as researcher—rather than rationally and explicitly standardized to be consistent across human beings. (See Wolcott, 1990, and Richardson, 1990, for their perspectives on this topic; review the theses of Marilyn and Chris, for example.) Past work offers less a map to novice researchers than an abundance of possibilities. Sensing the level of challenge ahead and having a sense of one's own strengths and limitations seems a prudent beginning.

QUESTIONS

4. How willing are you to "hold off" on questions about form and structure in order to see what your study "suggests" to you?

5. Do some areas of interest or disciplines, "beg" for qualitative research?

6. Can thinking about a traditional dissertation structure facilitate your understanding of a research project's "whole?" If so, how?

7. One of Marie's goals was to "guide readers … through the learning/research process I had gone through." Is that also a goal of qualitative research? Is that a goal for you?

8. What is your level of knowledge and experience with current qualitative research theory and practice? What else do you need to know?

9. Traditionally, the modal number of chapters in a dissertation is 5; what is the norm at your institution? In your department? Does it matter?

10. How much control do the student, faculty members, and graduate school have in determining the appearance and style of the thesis? Which decisions, if any, are negotiable?

11. Do you know how much writing is involved? Are your committee members aware of how much reading is involved?

12. Is the goal of the dissertation to provide a piece of research for committee approval, for publication, or both? Are the respondents an intended audience? Do different audiences require different presentations, formats, and structures? Different information? Whom will you please? Whom must you please?

WRITING, PART ONE

If we focus on the format of the dissertation in terms of the number of chapters, it is clear we still know very little about HOW the substance and style of the effort evolved into that particular format. Several of the correspondents offered vague clues into their process; for instance, the format "sort of emerged appropriate to the content" and "no other form made sense." What is less vague is the concept that novice qualitative researchers are also making decisions as writers.

The Writing Sequence

Jane, who sent me regular updates during her dissertation research, describes the writing of her thesis this way:

> I sent [my advisor] partly completed drafts of chapters 1,3,4 and an outline of chapter 2 and some ideas for chapter 5. It was my intent to show the big picture of where I think the study is headed. My advisor appreciated that and said the way I was writing was intriguing—inside out, backwards, and all over the place! I can't imagine working this kind of project any other way. I now have a much better sense of what exactly to include in my literature review, for example, and I really couldn't have known that until a great deal of findings were written up. Actually, it seems that the findings chapter (4) is in the best shape of all the chapters! Because I now understand what the study is looking like, I can go back and refine the other chapters. I guess I have resisted accepting that kind of a process because it's so contrary to "traditional" experimental designs! But it's really what has worked with me.

One reviewer of this book commented that the writing of traditional dissertations also follows the pattern Jane suggests. Maybe so, but one of the things that captured my attention in Jane's description is the advisor's sense of intrigue: What is the level of understanding about a process such as Jane's, where the doing, reporting, analyzing, focusing, and writing do not combine or necessarily come together in a linear fashion? Does Jane's description explicate the characteristics of interaction among these processes in such a way that a sense of intrigue can be replaced with support of and for the processes? I think so. Jean's experience parallels Jane's.

> The last chapter I wrote was the methodology chapter. I wrote the chapters out of order—with the understanding and support of two writers with whom I was working [Jean's respondents]. One ..., who acted as my cheerleader, good friend, and confidant, assured me at one point that all writers write what they can at the moment. I must say that the members of my committee came to understand my position and process. I wrote the conclusions before I wrote the balance of the 5th chapter.

> The "conclusions" are within the bodies of chapters 4 and 5 and also in the final chapter. I do not like the word conclusions and did not wish to use it in my dissertation. My committee was comfortable with that.

Style Options and Requirements

Like format considerations, writing style may be a matter of personal preference or an issue over which you have no control. One anonymous correspondent chose to write "in third person, but only because it 'sounded right.'" Marie builds a stronger case for her choices:

> I was a fairly good writer and quite analytical, which may have helped. I told my committee I was going to use a first person narrative and justified doing so using the social science literature I had discovered myself, quoting also from Don Graves, Paul Woodring, and a few others who were calling for educational research to be written with a human voice. I stated that as my goal was to bring about change, I was going to write my research so that those individuals at the site could not only read it but also have enough of a vicarious sense of the methods I described writers using that they could imitate these methods if they chose. My depart-

ment valued clear prose writing with a strong personal
voice.

Like Marie, I was also able to make decisions about writing style. The
decisions were connected to a sense of how certain pieces of the dissertation needed to be presented in order to support my conception of the
"whole."

> Chapter 1 introduces the study. The chapter is written in the
> third person, because the ideas incorporated in the thesis
> exist in the current literature of inquiry, organizations, and
> education.

> Chapter 2 contains eight interview case reports. Each is
> written in narrative form in order to provide you with a
> sense of the interview interaction as it occurred. This chap-
> ter provides the database from which chapter 3 is derived
> …

> Chapter 3 is the final analysis of the interview data. This
> chapter is written in the first person, because it is my inter-
> pretations focused by the purposes of the study. I strongly
> urge you to refer to Chapter 2 and to your own sense of the
> eight case reports in order to determine the accuracy and
> possibility of the interpretations….

> Chapter 4 presents four hypotheses about organizing….
> The thesis and the methodology together generated the
> content from which the hypotheses are derived. (Meloy,
> 1986, pp. v–vi)

Through this research, I have found individuals who enjoyed deci-
sion-making freedoms similar to my own. However, there are as many who
did not. For example, one of the correspondents remembers "tense" as a
style and power issue.

> The biggest problem I had was writing in the past tense. My
> major professor wanted me to use past tense rather than

present tense. During my first course, the professor insisted that students in the department write using the present tense. As a result, I relearned to write research papers using the present tense (for example, "Moore claims" rather than "Moore claimed".) I utilized this 'new writing technique' for 3 years. For my dissertation, my major professor required that I use past tense, stating that some of the authors of my references were dead and that was about as past tense as one can get. Ha! Ha! So of course, I us_ed_ past tense!

Another correspondent's advisor also had the final say.

My advisor was adamant about the need to use 3rd person and passive voice. I made a strong case for writing in a more interesting style, but my advisor found that too "chatty" and insisted on an almost mechanical traditional research style. The resulting dissertation is a sure cure for insomnia.

Qualitative Researchers as Writers

Even more than the correspondents for the first edition, the additional writers for this volume have convinced me through their work that qualitative researchers most often not only like to write but also must be able to write well. Perhaps it is because of this characteristic that the question of the "articulate I" as creator of fiction or presenter of fact remains unresolved (Meloy, 1995). Although qualitative researchers and scholars are continuing to define and refine what qualitative researchers do, the resulting representations as either stories or research remains a topic under discussion (e.g., Barone, 1992a, 1993; Carter, 1993; Clandinin & Connelly, 1996). The point I wish to make here is simply that as a novice researcher, you will by necessity of the process either become a writer or mature as one. Jean writes:

My son just came in to tell me how easy I made writing look.... Writing does not come easily for me, although I think of myself as a writer and usually use a legal pad and pencil when I write, transferring my first draft to the computer—revising it then and then again, and so forth. I am composing this at the computer so I know it rambles and is not "tight." I face the terror of the blank page just like any other writer when I am supposed to be writing and the words don't flow.

Actually I LOVE writing and look at the blank page as an invitation. One of the wonderful "results" or "conclusions" that I have taken away from the experience of writing a dissertation … is that I KNOW I am a member of the club of writers. Writers really are people. PEOPLE who write. I also feel a certain sense of accomplishment that NO ONE can take away from me.

Figures

Only one correspondent mentioned developing figures for the thesis.

The figures created a huge <u>HEADACHE</u>. The ones within the second chapter were relatively easy to create. I am blessed with a wonderful husband who is a whiz on the computer. He used the computer facilities at work to create those figures for me. They looked as though they had been done by a professional draftsman. The other figures evolved. I was and still am extremely frustrated by the constraints put on figures by University Microfilms. Because I was doing original research neither my chair nor the "chief nitpicker" at the Graduate School could offer much assistance. (I should be nicer about the person at the Graduate School responsible for dissertations. She was only doing her job. She is the person who uses a light table to look for typeovers and a ruler to measure margins.) I learned—the hard way—to get absolutely everything in writing. I had all of the figures done and took them to the lady at the Graduate School who told me that they all had to be redone. I cried for hours over the cost and the time "lost."

Looking at the final form of qualitative dissertations will provide examples of the structures their authors used to organize their final sense of the research focus. The thesis may appear neat and tidy, but that final appearance seems to be an artifact of the research process rather than an a priori signpost the researcher followed. This concept can be particularly troublesome for those of us who were taught to outline beginning with Roman numeral I. The processes of pulling together, sifting, organizing, and writing our thoughts are a challenge, because the coming together occurs in nonlinear, halting, and multiple ways. The task of choosing which strands to pursue, when and how, as well as how to organize them and write them up is a recurring and difficult one. Even though it seems what Paul Simon sings is true, "the nearer your destination the more you're slip-sliding away," the correspondents' reflections provide a measure of comfort for the processes of researching and writing, thinking and doing.

QUESTIONS

13. What is your writing style? Is your writing clear? Do others understand your writing? Do you like to write?

14. If your writing style just "seems right," what does that mean? Just right for what? Can you explain its sense to someone else? Do models exist to support your style preference? Are such efforts necessary to justify your own? Why or why not?

I would like to pose several additional questions that come from my particular educational background and research experiences. I ask them because I am trying to answer them for myself. I think the issue of why we do what we do and how we represent the resulting constructions is linked to the larger issue surrounding our decision to use qualitative or quantitative methodologies in our research.

QUESTIONS

15. Is qualitative research the result of a qualitative method? What makes a study qualitative? What assumptions are being made? How does anyone's writing reflect those assumptions?

16. Does writing reflect an "either–or," that is, a "quantitative" or "qualitative" mindset? Is there such a thing? Is this important to consider? If methods are combined, can writing approaches be combined? Can "qualitative" writing be quantitative? What assumptions do we make about writing, description, numbers, pictures, poetry, and so forth?

SUMMARY

The excerpts from the correspondents' letters begin to illuminate the sense of <u>not</u> knowing what will happen until you get there. A major sensemaking strategy is ambiguity reduction (Weick, 1979; 1995). Qualitative researchers continuously make more and more, rather than fewer and fewer, decisions. It is only at the point of closure to a qualitative research experience (and even then there is most likely no flashing red light or octagonal sign) that the complex, layered experience in which we engage begins to take shape as a sensible "whole" that can be—and indeed has been—organized, interpreted, and perhaps understood. Theses do not emerge all at once; if the thesis is qualitative, chances are it will not arrive headfirst. Understanding follows doing. However, as the correspondents suggest, the dissertation will indeed develop in a way congruent with perceived purposes, an understanding of methodological issues, and interaction with one's committee. In order to describe how such coherence comes about, the remaining chapters of this book are presented in a rough linear sequence in the order in which doctoral students might encounter them. Within this attempt at order, I will also try to draw attention to the ongoing, multilayered sensemaking inherent in the role of qualitative researcher as the human research instrument. Although we can know more than one thing at one time, our ability to communicate multiple understandings simultaneously remains limited. I believe this book can promote multiple understandings through the senses or connections it makes with you, the reader. As such, I'll end—and begin—with a lengthy excerpt from Barbara, whose reflection on the undertaking begins with her introduction to research.

I'd like to begin by sharing a passage that I wrote a year ago (December 1997) while taking a research course. As a requirement, we had to conduct a small research project.

What follows are my initial findings, thoughts, and feeling about the research process:

Review and Retrieval of the Research, was my first initiation into this mysterious realm, and I emerged with an understanding of the *general* definitions of Positivist, Interpretive, and Alternative research. I could now use these terms with a fair amount of authority but had only begun to understand their deeper meanings. Now, having completed my second research course—*Alternative Paradigms*—I have a still clearer grasp of research paradigms and methodologies, yet I am realizing that the more I learn, the more there is to learn.

While driving to the supermarket the other day, I began rolling some words and phrases around in my head; language that comes up often in the readings: ethnomethodology, hegemony, epistemologies, empiricism, post-modernism, neo-Marxist, Friereian, participatory, subjectivity, and so forth, and I have conflicted feelings about these words and phrases. Although I understand the meanings of these academically charged phrases and can use them intelligently in conversation (a good feeling), I often feel trivial and uncomfortable using this new language.

This raises questions for me: Who is qualified or authorized to speak this elite language, the language that separates one from the *other*, the researcher from the participant(s)? *Whose* language is this? It is not the language that I used in my home growing up and is therefore a new language, something that I can put on and subsequently take off. This is the language that I speak in the classroom and with other doctoral students, but it is not the language that I use in my personal life, and therefore it seems separate and false and almost humorous, as if I live a dual existence. It is a secret language spoken by a secret society.

Another wholly unexpected feeling arises each time I sit down to write my field notes. It is a feeling that seems silly now that I am removed from it (writing the field notes). Yet when I sit and write I feel as if I am involved in a clandestine operation, shrouded in secrecy. I think about my partici-pant(s) as I write and I know that they are unaware that I am at home writing about them, regardless of the fact that I have their permission to observe and interview them, and I feel covert, like a spy. From a human emotional perspective there seems to be something unnatural about this research, yet from an academic perspective I understand its purpose...

Judy, since then, I have completed my doctoral level course work, passed my qualifying comprehensive examinations, and am in the process of collecting the data that will be-come my dissertation. *To revisit what I wrote a year ago is to be reminded of the general discomfort that I felt about conducting research, which has influenced the methodol-ogy that I've chosen for my dissertation.* [italics added]

In my study I recognize that I am most qualified to analyze the depictions of those characters that I identify with.... However, in my attempt to be inclusive, I am deliberately including all groups....

This approach begins to resolve my initial dilemma with the notion of research being an exclusive activity—con-ducted in clinical laboratory settings by the scientist who studies the "others." The research must be meaningful to me in emotional ways, as well as in scientific, scholarly, and intellectual ways....

I do belong to a doctoral group that meets once a month in the home of one of our professors. This has been a significant factor in my doctoral experience, [having] a support group in a private setting away from academia.

Barbara's writing doesn't stop here. In Appendix C, Barbara continues to discuss her methodological choices. You will experience Barbara's sensemaking as it occurs while she was writing to me. The follow-up letter exemplifies the thinking, reflecting, writing, interpreting, and coming to know that is qualitative research.

3

UNDERSTANDING
AT THE BEGINNING

Selecting and Working With
a Committee and Advisor

My committee also recognized the necessity of risk taking, encouraged and supported me in it, and took risks that seem at times to have been greater than the risks I took. My dissertation was, in many ways, a collaboration of the group, nurtured by my advisor's commitment to political activism, allowed to expand in its own way as I "became" a PhD. (Marilyn)

One of the original focusing questions for this book asked correspondents to comment on their "negotiations" with their committee members. Fortunately, the correspondents mostly ignored the probe and wrote what they wanted to about this topic. They praise faculty from several institutions and representing a variety of disciplines for their support, advice, knowledge, and interest. They also offer many practical suggestions to novice dissertation writers, from having a sense of direction about one's own work to establishing working relationships of mutual respect. Correspondents recent and past will tell you that the role of the faculty member—as advisor, chair or committee member—is crucial to intellectual, psychological, and emotional satisfaction.

A SENSE OF DIRECTION

Ann not only asserts knowledge of the faculty members she chose for her committee but also offers a clear sense of the qualitative direction of her work.

> Three people made up my committee. My advisor's re-
> search interest made me want to attend the university I
> chose. One of the two other committee members was an in-
> dividual with whom I had a 2-year research assistantship.
> The third taught in my minor area, and I got to know this
> person, an anthropologist, through a course I took. I knew
> all three of these people respected the qualitative tradition
> in which I chose to work. Each have conducted or orga-
> nized interview studies. All respected my research per-
> spective.

Patricia describes the timing of and expectations for her committee selection. "I picked my graduate committee after I had begun my researches
and selected both data gathering and analytical techniques. I point-blank
asked potential committee members about any biases they had concerning
qualitative approaches." Jane asserts herself even more forcefully.

> I CHOSE A COMMITTEE FULLY COGNIZANT THAT
> I WANTED NOTHING BUT A QUALITATIVE
> DESIGN; I ONLY ASKED FACULTY TO BE ON MY
> COMMITTEE WHOM I KNEW ENDORSED THE
> METHOD! (I guess that's clear....)

Ann, Patricia, and Jane assert the importance of knowing the subject area
and methodological predispositions of potential committee members. Linda,
who conducted an interdisciplinary study, writes that because she "already
had a vision" of what she wanted to pursue, the home department of her thesis
was less an infringement on her focus than it might have been. She continues:
"If I hadn't been at a relatively nontraditional institution, in a relatively nontraditional department, supported by a wonderful chair and good friends in a
dissertation support group, I probably would not have survived the process."

Jean spends a good part of one letter describing her committee members.
Among the many themes suggested in the selection that follows, I was interested in the number of ways the various backgrounds and expertise of
committee members can support a dissertation research experience.

> I'd like to give you a bit of background on my committee. I
> was able to select four members of my committee (my

chair and three others). The fifth member of my committee was appointed by the Graduate School and was someone from outside of my department. That person's job is
as the Graduate School's watchdog—to be sure that all
procedures were followed to the letter of the law, "*i*'s"
dotted and "*t*'s" crossed. That person may also contribute.
The outside member is assigned on a rotating basis from a
pool of all the members of the graduate faculty. He or she
can be anyone. I did not know the man assigned, but his
understanding of my subject matter and what I wanted to
do was very helpful.

My chair is a writer and edits a journal of qualitative research. He was kind and helpful and willing to admit he'd
never done anything quite like what I was trying to do. I
know I tried his patience more than once.

Another committee member is my mentor and friend. We
had worked as collaborators (and continue to do so). She
understands my writing process and was able to help me
"cut and paste" in ways that my chair was not. Her chair
had helped her through this writing experience, so she was
able to pass the learning on to me. (I miss her being just
down the hall. It is not easy collaborating with someone
who is several hundred miles away. I must say that my
phone bill has been a bit steep since my family's move.)

Another committee member was a department chair. I had
known this person as a teacher and friend. His research
skills were invaluable; he protected me from myself and
from another member of my committee when he felt that
person's requests were out of line. He and another faculty
member in my department (who is a GEM!) taught me how
to use the phrase: "I am sorry but <u>that</u> is beyond the scope of
my dissertation."

Another faculty member was able to help me in many ways, because she had done her graduate work with an important researcher in my field. Finally, I also received a great deal of help from an anthropologist who teaches at the university. Because the materials I used were more like artifacts, her knowledge of anthropology and methodology were helpful.

Diana's reflection mirrors a part of Jean's:

In retrospect, I must say that the primary reason I "chose" Beth was personal rather than academic. Our research interests are similar, but even more importantly, I was immediately impressed by Beth's ability to listen, encourage, and help me clarify my own ideas. The fact that we continue to work together more than 2 years after my dissertation was completed illustrates our relationship well.

I cannot leave Ellen out here:

My committee chair, Dr. Gaalen Erickson, is a veteran scholar, who learned along with and mentored his students to take educated risks necessary to one's objectives. Largely due to this professor's understanding and help along with a collaborative committee, I was able to develop and publish the Multiple Intelligence Teaching Approach (MITA) model I now use.

Dana sums it up this way:

If I were to give advice on selecting committee members, I would say this. First and foremost, choose people who believe in you. Choose people who are respectful of you as an adult human being with a life outside the university. Choose people who can clearly identify next steps, and, if possible, energize you about taking them. If those people recognize doctoral study as both sublime and ridiculous, they are rare finds who should be cultivated as mentors.

RESPECT

Concomitant with knowing your own interests and the preferences and strengths of potential committee members is the issue of mutual respect and faculty confidence in your abilities. For example, one anonymous correspondent piqued my curiosity by writing, "What I had to negotiate with my committee was mainly my freedom of thought and action, which they were willing to give me once I had gained their confidence. Each of the five members of my committee was excellent and inspirational." I wrote back, asking for specific details on "gaining the confidence" of the committee. A brief time later, I received the following reply:

> You have asked how I gained my committee's confidence, which I recommended as contributing to the success of my thesis experience. After entering graduate school, I observed early on that those PhD candidates least anxious about completing their theses were those with supportive and protective mentors, students who were also keeping close contacts with their other committee members and facilitating close contacts between them. I learned that students almost always initiate these close and productive student–committee relationships, and that everyone involved in the productive relationship had learned to respect one another. It is the task of the student to nurture the mutual respect that bears fruit (the thesis). It is most important for the student to demonstrate scholarly competence in small ways over a long period of time; for example, by undertaking independent studies with prospective committee members that require readings, research, and a written report—and then, by attempting to get the research report published somewhere. This takes many semesters to accomplish, but with patience and luck students can earn the confidence of those faculty who will provide them ultimately with a positive thesis experience. When the time ar-

rives to begin writing the thesis, the student may enjoy the unexpected freedom to act independently of close faculty supervision. This situation allows a student creativity in thesis preparation that otherwise might not be tolerated. This is only possible, of course, because of hard-won committee confidence.

Maria, in an excerpt from a longer letter discussing the importance of a dissertation study group to her experience (see chap. 5), wrote explicitly about respect.

As we [the study group] worked, we chose our committee members with care. My advisor and another of her colleagues, both of whom received degrees from the same university, were on my committee. I needed two other members and chose two faculty members (one in my program and one outside my program) whom I knew would be supportive of my efforts, because they respected me and my work. This may sound immodest, but members of the study group had already established their reputations as conscientious students who did quality work. We chose committee members who were willing to go along with our ideas (at least initially), because they respected us.

We also picked committee members who we thought would be intellectually open to the idea of qualitative research. It was not possible to have all committee members fit these criteria, because of the substance of some of the studies. We tried (and succeeded), however, to weight the committee membership with basically supportive faculty.

Faculty members have opportunities in class to make an impression on students. Making a solid impression on faculty members appears to be an equally important thing to do.

Jean points out that an *environment* for interactions of mutual respect is also important.

I believe that one of the strengths of the Center for Teaching
and Learning's doctoral program ... is its insistence that
candidates select their own topics and their own committees (with the exception of the faculty member appointed
by the Graduate School). Individual faculty members and
members of the committee provide guidance. They challenge the candidate to consider possibilities; they offer articles, essays, and books; "nudge" or "nag" about deadlines;
but avoid "telling" the candidate what to do. They believe
in self-directed learning and risk taking. They urge candidates to become actively involved in their own learning.
They recognize that unless a candidate is self-directed and
sees relevance in what is being studied, the learning won't
be the same. They model and practice what they teach.
There are hurdles that doctoral candidates must jump. A
self-directed learner–risk taker jumps higher and more persistently.

The first set of questions in this chapter came to mind as I was thinking,
"How fortunate some students and faculty members are!" Having specific
interests or locating oneself at a particular university for particular purposes seems a smart thing to do, especially because that was not indicative
of my initial approach to doctoral studies. Another correspondent writes:

Judy, Here are my responses to your questions. They are
honest and from my soul.... I decided to get a doctorate for
several reasons, most of them not highly intellectual or academic. I liked the ceremonial garb worn by PhD graduates.
I liked the cool tams and the lavish robes with stripes. I like
the aura that surrounds a newly anointed PhD—it's an air
of confidence, of knowledge, of having set out to accomplish a goal and actually fulfilling it. It's pure, and it's
sweet. I wanted that. I decided at the graduation ceremony
when I received my MA to pursue my PhD.

Such a trivial reason will not sustain one in such a lofty endeavor. I needed substance. It needed to be personal. I de-

cided to pursue a doctorate because of a professor in my masters program. She had a doctorate, and I wanted to pattern myself after her. She was my idol and my role model—I wanted to be like her. I needed a PhD.

I chose this institution because it was nearby; I could get accepted, having done my undergraduate and graduate work there; I was working full-time at a small private college in the area; and because I wasn't willing to take a risk and leave all things familiar.

QUESTIONS

1. Why did you choose to earn a doctorate? Do your reasons influence your choice of study, methodology, commitment? How much time are you willing to spend on this effort?

2. How did you select your university? Did you know what you wanted to do and with whom you wanted to work? Will the choices you have made support your dissertation research endeavor?

3. Do you know how doctoral students are viewed at your institution? In the department? As students? Co-learners? Does it matter to you?

4. What assumptions are you making about potential committee members? Have you read their work? Had a class with them? Heard about them? What do you need to know about them? How will you find out? What do they need to know about you? How will they find out?

5. Have you established a respectable "track record" of academic performance?

6. Can you assess the level of respect between you and the faculty members with whom you would like to work?

7. Do you have the sense that your faculty members are also learners? Do they have the sense that you are one?

QUALITATIVE–QUANTITATIVE

During doctoral study, idealistic purposes of thinking and learning can give way to practical realities as individuals pursue their futures through their present day choices. Sometimes those choices are based on a priori knowledge and experience; sometimes they are not. What happens when a student has only a general sense of his or her purposes and the next steps, the choice and availability of faculty members is limited, or the student inadvertently ends up with a nonsupportive faculty member? One correspondent candidly admitted the following:

> If I am to be honest, the committee was formed with little real understanding of the consequences that would result from individual selection.

> My department had only recently developed a PhD program, and two committee members were a "given," the department chairman and the Dean of the School of Education. The department chairperson was no problem, while the Dean was a "quant" to the extreme, often remarking how the dissertation had to be 'formal' and 'real research' (different from my approach).

For the first edition, the quantitative–qualitative aspects of committee selection were a major source of ambiguity. Gretchen recalls:

> Graduate committees must come in all combinations of expertise. I had no quantitative "experts" on mine, although three of the four members had done some quantitative studies. My dissertation director encouraged a qualitative approach with triangulation provided by also including quantitative tables (more about that later). Other committee members included the faculty member who teaches field research methods, a specialist in my subject area and the 'outside' person who was actually the most helpful of all, because he taught evaluation using Guba and Lincoln (1981; 1989) as the course textbook.

I now wish that I had included someone who was <u>expert</u> in quantitative studies as a part of my committee. I have had to redo all the statistical analyses to meet the requirements of journal reviewers; what my committee accepted is not accepted by others.

Gretchen's comments provide a clear example of how many issues of concern to doctoral students intermingle. In order to stay with the immediate topic, two correspondents offer the following suggestions to those of you less clear about the implications of your methodological choices. Both Lew and Tim suggest: "Talk to (screen) potential committee members. As a student, you may not understand the gap between qualitative and quantitative; talking to faculty members about what you might want to do will help." Tim adds: "My experience with quantitative-positivist oriented professors has been pretty good…. Quantitative researchers are not ignorant or inherently evil. Students should appeal to their intellectual curiosity."

One of the reviewers of this book suggested that the current arena for dissonance appears to be less the quantitative–qualitative paradigm struggle than the methodological differences among the variety of approaches to qualitative research. Paula agrees:

One thing that is in my journal is the question of whether I should call my study "qualitative research" or "naturalistic inquiry." Isn't there a quote out of Shakespeare, "What's in a name?" I felt that if I could put a name on the kind of research, then I would know better what rules to follow. I think these terms need to be better defined for students. Are they the same? I am not a qualitative researcher; at the time, I was a student trying to complete a dissertation. Maybe researchers know the differences among terms, but I don't. The literature, which I read, did not deal very well with this issue, although some of the authors tried to handle it. Let's define some terms for students and for faculty who are used to working with quantitative studies.

I believe our "divergences" have become more clearly articulated during the past ten years (e.g., see Creswell, 1998), however, none of the correspondents for the second edition suggested this emphasis as a concern.

SUMMARY

In the case of my own dissertation, by the time I was ready to prepare and defend the proposal and select the final committee, my methodological background was well-established. Having taken a full load of research courses—a seemingly endless sequence of statistics and design courses, qualitative inquiry courses, and courses on theory building and evaluation—I was able to "appeal" to at least one quantitatively oriented professor in part because I could explain the differences between what I proposed to do and how a study using an a priori framework would vary from that. Although I believe qualitative research stands on its own merits, I felt it was necessary for <u>me</u> to ground my methodological choice in a solid under-standing of the options available. <u>I still believe that understanding one's methodological framework and its implications—from "problem" conception to final representation—is a necessary and important aspect of learning how to do qualitative research well</u>. I also think mutual respect can be earned by being able to speak "more than one language" and then to argue effectively for the strengths of one's choices. Kathy was just one of the correspondents who also thought about this issue:

> Many committee chairs are learning about qualitative dissertations along with their students as they make collaborative decisions. The research experience and background of each of these people and the relationship they have developed during the time the student was in the graduate program affect decisions made. Sometimes there is a common knowledge base; sometimes there isn't. The student at yesterday's session who is working with her third major professor is one extreme. Students who have done research collaboratively throughout their doctoral program are at the other. Some of us get feedback and input from other committee members. Others do not. The process can be an emotional one for both the student and the professor.

QUESTIONS

8. What are the local guidelines or requirements, if any, for selecting a committee? What would be the pluses and mi-

nuses of any one particular faculty member? Topic? Methodology? What is worth it to you?

9. Are there people in your department or college who can support your decision making around committee selection?

10. How many committee members must you have? Is the committee for the proposal the same one for the thesis? Who "picks" the outside committee member? Are there any Graduate School requirements? Department requirements?

11. Do you know where qualitative research expertise is the norm? Is it in your university? Discipline? Does that matter?

12. What are the pluses and minuses of having a quantitative researcher on your committee? What (or whom) do you need to be "successful" as you define it? When is a critic useful? What kinds of criticism can you take? Can you define the kind of help you need? Do you know which kind of support any individual faculty member may or may not be able to give?

13. Is it necessity to understand the variety of "qualitative" approaches? Is your approach methodologically, ideologically, philosophically grounded? Can you explain its nuances? Should you have to?

FACULTY–STUDENT LEARNING

Whether there is a "quant" on a committee seems less essential than that a student is able to work with others, both students and faculty members, who are knowledgeable. If Kathy is correct in her summary excerpted earlier, then the range in the levels of knowledge and the ability to support graduate student efforts vary from individual to individual, institution to institution. Pam writes:

My first survey research course was taught in an exploratory fashion. One half of the semester was for qualitative inquiry; one half for quantitative. I performed equally well in both, but my passion and excitement for qualitative research was easy to spot. My advisor was supportive, but not at all experienced as a qualitative researcher; I negotiated a comp exam that did not include a quantitative component, the first ever for any student in our department.... Our relationship as "colleagues" may have had something to do with that. My maturity for the "system" and knowing what I wanted, and what a "right" process looked like also contributed positively.

More important than the variability, perhaps, are some examples of what is being done about it. In an excerpt from a lengthy first letter, Maria describes the interactive learning that can occur among students and faculty and how a mutual faculty–student learning environment supports a graduate student's possibilities for doing a solid piece of research.

One of the things that fascinated me about the experience of the study group was the learning that occurred among faculty. I was the first member of the group to defend my overview and dissertation. I perceived that during both meetings, my advisor played a "teaching" role with the two "outside" committee members. I don't mean by this that he defended my work for me, but rather he placed my work within the larger context of interpretive research. At strategic moments, he stepped in and gave the other committee members the language they needed to discuss my dissertation within the interpretive paradigm. He modeled for them what were appropriate questions.... I believe he was able to do this because of his personal style and the respect and stature he had with the other committee members. Now, here's what is fascinating to me. During my defense, one member of my committee asked questions that were not appropriate to the interpretive paradigm. He subsequently served on the committees of other study group members. As he participated in later meetings, <u>he</u> was the one who began to "correct" other faculty members who were asking inappropriate questions. In short, he learned from my advisor and the members of the study group and then began educating other faculty. We saw this happen with several other faculty within our program who served on more than one of our committees....

As we went along, not only were the faculty and committee members learning, so were we. We learned from each other what questions to anticipate and how to articulate the rationale for what we were doing. The success of our learning was demonstrated, I believe, by the fact that several study group members did not have to make a single revision in their final documents. They were able to present the research method, rationale, and results with such clarity and precision, committees accepted the dissertations as written.

Robert recalls his experience around student-committee learning this way:

Your questions in the area of analysis reminded me of how important it was to educate my committee. They learned about emergent hypotheses, categories, field methods, grounded theory, and other concepts and jargon the qualitative researcher lives with daily. As long as I appeared to have a grasp on the methods, the committee was satisfied with the analysis. (I found I was my harshest critic in this area. Although I was satisfied that the methods were good and that themes were emerging, I kept an abiding/nagging feeling that what I observed was prejudiced by biases I was unable to account for. In essence, I questioned my own integrity....)

The only point I had to negotiate with the committee was the "so what." I was required to convince them that the exercise was as important as the results. Because my study was the first of its kind to be undertaken at my university, it was critical that my blueprint was readable—that this was as important as the conclusions that emerged proved challenging.

At this time, I want to offer an aside about the writing and reading of this book. After deciding it would not be enough to simply offer a book of letters (in other words, acknowledging that I undertook the research with some purpose in mind), a major frustration became the selecting and placement of particular letters and excerpts within the book. Each excerpt, no matter how focused the author seemed to be, usually contains more than one idea or issue. One characteristic qualitative researchers share, as Robert suggests, is the almost constant questioning of their choices. Decision making is a process that constantly refines and defines our "product." I know I said this was not a book of imperatives, but if I may offer one, it is that you do not let the choices I make stop you from discovering and discussing other issues of importance to you!

Faculty–student learning was a major focus in the first edition. Since that time, I also conclude from conversations and e-mail from students around the world that Pat's experience, which is the next excerpt, remains salient. She describes how she and her committee began to learn about qualitative research. Her experience is unlike any other of the correspondents. I am impressed that a university would provide the opportunity she describes. I also realize it will be some time before qualitative researchers are the "norm" in all disciplines at all institutions of higher education.

> My department did not know what or which way would be the most appropriate for a nontraditional dissertation. Outside "experts" from the University of Florida and the University of Tennessee were brought to the campus to lecture and conduct individual research appointments. The department chairperson or my committee chairperson was present at these appointments. My dissertation was developed through individual research appointments. At the first appointment, Rodman Webb from Florida State approved of the research project. At the second appointment, Kathleen Bennett (now Kathleen deMarrais) from the University of Tennessee made format suggestions that resulted in the chapter layout for my dissertation. I took her suggestions because they made sense to me.

Justifying Qualitative Research

"Educating the committee" remains a real-life experience for some neophyte qualitative researchers. Several correspondents honed in on the lack of a shared tradition in qualitative research at their institutions (remember Paula's comments), feeling they had to justify any alternative approach. Patricia, perhaps unknowingly, makes the issue explicit:

> I was fortunate in having a dissertation advisor who had had a number of his students working with qualitative formats. His own work is often done in a qualitative mode, and thus, he has significant experience in justifying the legitimacy of these approaches.

Ann's interaction with her advisor illuminates the concern more directly:

> I did have a strong and supportive advisor who pushed me through, although I found the process a painful one. She said to me when I saw her in January, after she had read someone's completed dissertation with a long section justifying qualitative research, "Why do you all feel so guilty about qualitative research?" I'm not really sure why, but I think we are continually squaring ourselves with science and not just our committee.

Many of the correspondents for the second edition might agree with Ann's last sentence. As they describe in later chapters, much of their decision making was based on a need for sense and coherence, offering explanations—if not a "squaring" of one's self—of choices made. In spite of continuing interest in qualitative research, in spite of the stretches 21st-century doctoral students are making in the areas of presentation and representation (e.g., Brearly, 2000; Freeman, 2000), there remain existing or emerging issues that do not automatically support a doctoral student's interests. For example, one correspondent shared the following; I offer it here, because of the feeling it conveys:

Let me begin by admitting that I misinterpreted your prompt from the beginning. When I read "nontraditional," I thought experimental, as in experimental novel or poetry. I thought of a dissertation that experimented with the form, pushing the envelope, stretching the structure. I thought of a dissertation that proves an antithesis, disproves a thesis, offers several theses, is a narrative or an autobiography, etc. I thought of the work of Robert Coover, whose short stories begin and begin again, or the poetry of Lawrence Ferlinghetti, or asynchronous jazz. I thought of the dissertation I had not written, or rather had written but changed.

Remembering Our Lives

Things happen and influence our decisions. As Robert wrote earlier, "sometimes I'm my harshest critic." Sometimes we forget that the rest of our lives are happening at the same time as our doctoral studies. Correspondents for this edition will tell you not to forget. Susan writes:

> Judy, as I reflect today on what I wrote yesterday, I think I've told you about my life, not just the dissertation process. But for me the two are intricately connected—practically one in the same. Not that the dissertation was my life—quite the opposite. I chose to live life and, secondarily, complete a dissertation. I could have never done it the other way—it wouldn't have been worth it.

Connected to our "real" lives is Katie's explicit thinking that can be used to answer an often-asked question, "When is enough, enough?"

> Remember that this work is part of your life, but not your life's work. Qualitative research and writing can seem endless, boundless, and without borders. These characteristics appeal to one side of me, but I realized during my writing that they can also drag out one's thinking and writing process beyond a point that is helpful, practical, or even healthy. I think it is necessary to set some boundaries (e.g.,

limit the number of themes you will write about, limit the amount you read on a single topic, don't ask for feedback on everything).

I would remove the parentheses from around Katie's examples and, with the support of my advisor, use them to help me prioritize and manage my qualitative research efforts.

QUESTIONS

14. What is your current level of experience and knowledge of research methodologies and practice? Will your level of knowledge make a difference in what you choose to do? Should it?

15. As student or faculty member, have you gotten the education you need to do your job well—that is, do you know your stuff?

16. What does an experienced faculty member need to know to support students who select to do qualitative research for their dissertations? What are the current "norms'" of accepted practice? Should a student have to defend them?

17. Are you aware of your "whole life?" What benefits might be gained by doing qualitative research for your dissertation? What might be sacrificed? (see Emotional Journey, chap. 7)

It is difficult to leave this section without referring to Jean's thoughts on qualitative versus quantitative research. Although "historical" for many at this point, they express what many students have felt.

Is qualitative research getting a "bad rap" because it is viewed as easy? I think that it is somehow viewed as not as rigorous, because it does not involve statistics and all of the mumbo jumbo that goes with extensive statistical analysis.

There seems to be a mystique that surrounds and overvalues anything scientific, mathematical, or both. One of the

doctoral students in geology asked me—while I was a doctoral student—if I had to meet the same requirements to receive a PhD that she did. She was amazed to discover that
we had to meet the same requirements. She was surprised
to learn that I had to conduct original, creative research for
my dissertation and that I had to develop my own topic, etc.

If some doctoral students feel defensive about their decision to undertake qualitative research, then might it be less from the fact of their methodological choices per se as it is from the fact that they are inexperienced
researchers and methodologists, less able to explain and argue their
choices and less sure about knowing what they are doing and why? Tim
offers several suggestions, which make sense to me. "Have a concrete
idea about what qualitative research means to you. Until you are confident
in your understanding of what you are going to do and how you are going
to do it, you will never be certain if you are conducting the research prop-
erly." He continues:

Stress the importance of knowing both sides of the paradigm dialogue. Although Dr. Wolcott said qualitative researchers no longer needed to defend their paradigm in
addition to their research in theses and dissertations, he is
speaking from an educational research perspective, where
qualitative research is more accepted. Students should
know the assumptions of both the qualitative and quantitative perspectives to better define and defend their own
work. As long as their work is under the evaluative control
of researchers unsympathetic to qualitative research, qualitative researchers will have to defend their perspective as a
whole, if only to place their own work in context for their
reviewers.

The correspondents' reflections continue to focus attention on the fact
that the language, assumptions, practice, and products of qualitative research are neither common nor necessarily commonly accepted at colleges
and universities, or among faculty members and graduate students. I have a
different question for this topic. Even if methodologies and strategies become "common" from a faculty member's point of view, aren't doctoral

students—regardless of methodological perspective—expected to be able to defend their choices? I recall graduate school stories about individuals who did not do well at their final dissertation defense because they could not explain, in-depth, their choices surrounding their research designs, which were slightly complicated statistical analyses done by or with someone from another department who <u>understood</u> statistics. Perhaps, an "exhaustive review of the literature" is not as necessary as some other means—within the thesis or at the defense—of determining a student's knowledge and understanding of his or her choices? Maria's study group experience might be one such opportunity.

SUMMARY

Experience tells me that the qualitative–quantitative arguments have long since filtered down from the lofty level of articulate debate in the late 80s to the concrete level of implications for practice. When it comes to practice, novice researchers and faculty members less knowledgeable about qualitative research do not seem always to be working hand-in-hand to ensure a process and product of explicit, well-honed, and arguable integrity and thereby intrinsic value. The inherent power inequality between student–faculty member or new faculty member–tenured faculty member can shape theses research efforts in direct and significant ways. A correspondent for the second edition shares the following as a prelude to the next section of this chapter:

> As my advisor became more ill the other person took over more control. At one point he told me I couldn't consult anyone else outside of him without his approval. Because the research involved [others], I knew there was no one who understood all of these issues and I needed to be talking with them. At one point this same person told me he refused to work with me over the summer and also advised me to drop my topic because it was too complicated. He wanted me to do a survey.... This survey had been done at least six times over the past 15 years with the same result....
>
> My advisor was getting too sick and therefore was unable to control this person. I had to request a committee member

from another university be appointed to my committee. I
knew she had expertise in my areas of interest and in qualitative research. She agreed, but this made the guy mad. He
tried to convince other faculty members to abandon my
committee and told them I was incompetent. Finally, after
a year the university appointed a faculty member from a
different discipline who had expertise in qualitative research.

My committee was co-chaired by this new person. Only
three of the members had any real experience with qualitative research. They were strong enough to convince the
other two that I was doing it right. This took another 6
months....

Such a power dynamic continues to be problematic to the future of qualitative research, because the dissertation experience often sets the tone and es-
tablishes the template for future researchers and researches. Fortunately,
the optimism of the correspondents remains high. Katie writes:

As you probably gleaned from my remarks on background,
I did not enter the doctoral program knowing that I wanted
to do qualitative research. I remember that on the first day
of one class I identified myself as feeling aligned with both
quantitative and qualitative approaches, and projected that
I would use both in my dissertation. Although I still appreciate (some) quantitative studies, I have learned that I am at
heart a qualitative researcher. Moreover, it's becoming
harder and harder for me to identify topics that are *really*
meant for quantitative study. The older I get, the more I see
spaces between ideas, relationships between actions, and
thinking, emotion, and context between "results." I see
more and more possibilities for representation of one's
studies, in contrast with fewer and fewer "conclusive" findings. It's hard to see how any of these things can be measured in an "objective," quantitative sense. Once, when I

was searching for readings on caring and was walking back from the library, I happened to remember a small book of writings by Martin Buber (1958, 1987) that I had read in a religion class in college. I went right to the bookstore and bought the book, and miraculously, opened to a page I remembered. The subject of the piece was about different ways of considering a tree—mathematically, scientifically, as an object of art, as something in which one might find a relationship. That entry of Buber's, shown to me by some guide in my subconscious memory, came to symbolize ... how I think about qualitative research....

I contemplate a tree.

I can accept it as a picture: a rigid pillar in a flood of light, ...

I can feel it as movement: the flowing veins around the sturdy striving core, ...

I can assign it to a species and observe it as an instance, ...

I can overcome its uniqueness and form so rigorously that I recognize it only as an expression of the law ...

I can dissolve it into a number ...

Throughout all of this the tree remains my object and has its place and its time span, its kind and condition.

But it can also happen, if will and grace are joined, that as I contemplate the tree I am drawn into a relation, and the tree ceases to be an It....

Whatever belongs to the tree is included: its form and its mechanics, its colors and its chemistry, its conversation with the elements and its conversation with the stars—all this in its entirety. (pp. 56–58)

QUESTIONS

18. What is the political environment at your university, college, or in your department surrounding qualitative research? Will political, personal, or publication issues influence your methodological decision making? The appearance of your dissertation? Do you know? How can you find out?

19. How willing are you to experience self-doubt, to <u>not</u> know exactly what you are doing? How interested are you in figuring things out? Is qualitative research for you?

20. If your department is qualitative "resource" shy, what alternatives are available to support doing qualitative research?

21. Who will "control" which data are collected? What types of suggestions are reasonable? Based on which criteria? What jeopardizes the rigor and integrity of any type of study? Do you know?

22. Can you choose your compromises—that is, what are you willing to negotiate and what will you remain firm about? Is it important to know "what qualitative research means to you" or what qualitative research means?

COMMITTEE–STUDENT INTERACTION

The level of involvement an individual seeks throughout the dissertation experience depends on individual strengths, needs, and context. Some will operate almost independently, whereas others work more closely with their committees. Certain committees or advisors may want the doctoral student to "go it alone," whereas others may want frequent opportunity for feedback. Students may prefer a lot of feedback or choose to work alone until the material appears to be reasonably cogent. Tim agrees with and speaks for several other correspondents about this topic.

> When dealing with committee members I believe it is cru-
> cial to be in constant contact—work with them, show them
> what you are doing, make certain they are with you from
> the beginning.... Without such guidance, I would feel lost.
> More importantly, I would be setting myself up for some
> potential surprises when the thesis is submitted if I did not
> know the opinions and questions of my committee mem-
> bers throughout the research and writing period.

Constant contact may not always be possible, as Jane made sure to mention. "It's also significant to tell you that I live 500 miles from my chair! I
am unable to run to my chair with lots of little questions! Mostly I just solve
them!" Pam encourages you "to stay on campus as long as you can and finish before engaging in real work again, if possible."

Another correspondent importantly complicates the issue of the frequency of interaction between committee and student:

> In my case, it was not geography alone that determined
> contact. I knew my dissertation advisor would be my big-
> gest hurdle, so I sent draft copies. Only after numerous
> (and I do mean numerous) rewrites and when the disserta-
> tion was 75% done, did I solicit feedback from other com-
> mittee members. Also, I never shared only one chapter with
> my advisor; I sent several chapters at once, because my ad-
> visor needed to see how my ideas were developing across
> the whole dissertation.

Whether you are near or far to your committee, Dana offers a smart suggestion:

> Throughout the dissertation process, I kept a spiral note-
> book dedicated to meetings with my committee members. I
> took careful notes with exact quotations when possible. I
> was able to tell one committee member the advice that an-
> other had given me, review their comments at later dates,
> and read them consecutively and cumulatively. This note-
> book was invaluable to me. Juggling conflicting feedback

is often a problem for doctoral students, and this notebook helped me identify and address any inconsistencies.

The quantity and frequency of contact with your committee will be influenced not only by your particular needs but also the types of efforts both you and your committee members believe are necessary and are able to make. Jane offers a lesson learned by doing:

> It occurred to me that I have been conditioned—all through my schooling and even now in graduate school—to think that the teachers and professors had THE ANSWERS. Even now I have been tempted to want my chair to tell me THE WAY to do it. Old habits die hard! I keep reminding myself that there is not just ONE WAY, obviously a view inherent in qualitative research. I also realize that completing a dissertation is in part an exercise in learning to make decisions and trust one's own judgment.

Unlike the clear, a priori designs available for quantitative research, however, the latitude for individual decision making—indeed the myriad of choices—can be daunting for the novice qualitative researcher.

QUESTIONS

23. What amount, kind, and frequency of interaction does your committee expect? What do you expect? Who will initiate the contact?

24. How self-motivated are you? How long can you sustain?

25. Does your chair wish you to share your writing with all committee members from the very beginning or after he or she has the opportunity to provide some initial feedback?

26. How much feedback do you personally need? How much can you handle?

27. Will it matter which chapters you first solicit for feedback? Why or why not?

Student–committee interaction remains a dominant theme in the discussion of a successful thesis experience. Linda reflects: "I also had a most decent committee. I was lucky (or perhaps I chose well!)."

4

UNDERSTANDING
BY PROPOSING

Preparing and Defending

Identify your area(s) of interest as soon as possible in your program, and look for ways to link your papers, course readings, independent studies, comprehensive exam questions, etc., to this topic. (Katie)

The first piece of official writing usually shared with a committee is the dissertation proposal. The correspondents provide evidence of a variety of learning cultures, describing how they prepared the proposal and what they assumed and learned by doing it. They also share some concerns that only became apparent to them after the defense and acceptance of the proposal, when data collection and analysis were in progress. Pulling it together for presentation, however, is the first step.

PROPOSAL PRESENTATIONS

The excerpts below highlight the difficulty two correspondents experienced as they were "learning by doing." Carol recalls:

When I first wrote up the proposal, etc., I outlined the dissertation in a traditional quantitative way—problem, literature search, methodology, findings, conclusions. My committee laughed me out of the building. They let me know that qualitative research is different. It was okay to talk in the first person! And "real" qualitative research does not know what the thesis is until the interviews are done and analyzed.

Another correspondent also found the first proposal presentation to be less than successful.

> My first field study proposal was rejected flat by my advisor. It took another 6 months to enrich the original plan. The resulting study was much better.

> The addition of a priori hypotheses about demographic differences was something "tacked on" by my advisor at the last minute before the proposal was signed ... more with the view of providing publishable data than from a philosophical basis.

Still another correspondent offers some additional detail around the effort of developing and presenting the prospectus:

> After I decided on the topic for my dissertation, I spent several months reading the literature trying to find a theory or framework by which to interpret what I thought I might find! I put together a short proposal and distributed it to committee members. My chair does qualitative research, but of a more theoretical or secondary analysis bent. My chair was supportive of my approach and objectives in this first proposal, which involved testing a series of hypotheses....

> Another committee member, also of a qualitative orientation and whom I think was very wise said, "If this is what you really want to do, fine, I'll support it, but I think you'd have a better study if you took a more inductive approach...." Another committee member, who is a seasoned field researcher, said the same thing: "Just go and start hanging out in the setting and talk to everyone about everything and write down everything you observe and see what emerges as interesting. Don't worry about having an analytical framework at this point." (Quotes are not their exact words, but a paraphrase.)

So this is what I ended up doing, and I think it was an excellent decision. That is, I ended up approaching the study
much more inductively, with justification provided by soci-
ologists Glaser and Strauss (1967) in their volume *The Discovery of Grounded Theory*. This is an excellent but
densely written manifesto.... Schooled as I am in the de-
ductive method, I had some resistance to this approach (as
well as emotional anxiety as to "but what if nothing interesting appears?"), but of course it has, and I think my project will be much richer for having proceeded this way. As
it turns out, the focus is...

These reflections suggest some of the struggles past experience and un-
clear expectations foster as doctoral students begin to undertake a qualitative
research project. What makes me smile is the beginning of the last sentence in
the last excerpt. "As it turns out" has the familiar ring of several statements
made earlier, such as "I ended up with." The foci of qualitative research proposals emerge as a result of interaction in the research context; a priori ideas
give way to issues discovered there. Although novice qualitative researchers
are told that research foci "emerge," the last excerpt suggests how changes in
preparation and thinking enabled a particular focus to do so.

PROPOSAL MODELS

Course work, as well as committee member suggestions, can support the
writing of the proposal. Ann recalls:

When I wrote my (first) proposal, I was in a research methodology class. As well as preparing the class for the qualifying exam, the instructor required us to write a proposal.
In each class we presented our efforts toward finding a
question, preparing the method, and planning the literature
review. To stop those questions, "What does a proposal
look like?" and "How do I write one?" the professor distributed former students' successful proposals.

The proposal I subsequently completed was modeled on
these successful proposals, with a similar skeleton of state-

ment of purpose, literature review, methods, analysis section, and chapter outline of the dissertation. Only up to a point were these sample proposals helpful, however. As I understood my question better, I found that writing a proposal was a creative process—it became my proposal and no one else's....

At the beginning, but not during the writing, I found books such as Yin's (1984) helpful. It was too prescriptive later when I was well away into creating my proposal. After I finished my proposal and before the defense I found the books helpful to tighten certain sections (methodology and analysis) and to just generally prepare for the defense of the proposal.

I made it clear that my research question was well-grounded and of both practical and theoretical significance. I also tried to emphasize that my study was exploratory; my sample would be drawn....

Although no hypotheses were written into my proposal, I did find it helpful on my own to prepare a long list of hypotheses after I had conducted my pretest of the interview questions. I compiled this list partly because so many thoughts and speculations came out of those preliminary interviews and analysis and because I thought they might help guide and shape later analysis after data collection.

One of the themes that both interests and troubles me is the variety of ways the correspondents talk about qualitative research. Because of my education and subsequent understanding of qualitative research, words like "subjects" and "hypothesis" make me nervous. I think it makes sense to highlight this concern here, because the proposal process is at the beginning of the formal dissertation research experience. Most doctoral students are novice researchers; what they learn and begin to understand conceptually through their course work takes on additional and more concrete meaning in practice. Perhaps the time for the defense of a "qualitative" proposal ought to be later in the research process, after an initial investigation has been undertaken around a focusing idea? As several correspondents have already suggested, the selection of the committee and the clarification of the proposal came <u>after</u> they had spent some time in the research context, that is, after they had begun figuring out "the rules."

SUMMARY

Proposal writing doesn't appear to be something that comes naturally. We learn not only by example but also by the reactions and suggestions of committee members. The correspondents remember having just a tentative sense about what to do and how to do it. Preparing a proposal that can be successfully defended (substantively and methodologically) is one area that clear guidelines and examples can support.

QUESTIONS

1. What does a proposal look like? How might one that incorporates qualitative research methodologies differ from other models? Should it?

2. What is the role of theory in qualitative research? Are a priori theoretical frameworks and quantitative hypotheses compatible with your understanding, knowledge, and definition of qualitative research? How so? If not, why not?

3. Is it possible for a student to have an idea of what he or she wants to do but have no clear sense about how to get at it? Is this much ambiguity troublesome?

4. What do you believe your committee members' roles to be? What do they believe their roles are? Do you know?

5. Who is going to tell whom about what you are going to do? How much guidance do you expect? How much responsibility are you willing to take?

6. What does it mean to "create" a proposal? Where is the latitude (e.g., in substance and context), and where are the constraints (e.g., in methodological or theoretical frameworks)?

MORE ABOUT PROPOSING

Ambiguity

One question for faculty members that may be crucial is this: If we are in the position to tell students what to do (or accept what they suggest), then what are the implications for student research based on our knowledge or lack thereof? If we add the "newness" for the student of writing a proposal to the simultaneous "newness" of trying to figure out the ramifications of qualitative research, the sum is a certain amount of additional ambiguity within committee–student interactions.

Several correspondents suggested that understanding what we are doing while distinguishing and justifying the qualitative from the quantitative remained an issue in the early 1990s. Although this volume is presented somewhat horizontally across dissertation checkpoints, almost every excerpt contains more than one idea that would fit under more than one heading. The concept of "mutual simultaneous shaping" that Lincoln and Guba (1985) discussed appears to be an appropriate descriptor for the interactive processes and concurrent ambiguity the human being, as research instrument, experiences. Maria remarks on the difficulties posed by such ambiguity during the proposal defense:

> One of the difficulties in writing a proposal for interpretive research is the uncertainty surrounding the format and content of the results. We found it difficult to maintain the integrity of the inductive research process and still answer committee members' questions about our anticipated results.... As we gained more experience in writing overviews, we became more skillful in articulating the process that would lead to the final construal. My advisor also encouraged people to do pilot studies to collect some preliminary data so they could begin to get a sense of what the construal might be.

> One of the needs I had in developing both my proposal and dissertation was to articulate a rationale for what I was doing—essentially building an argument for the legitimacy of my research design.... My intent was to show that

grounded theory was, in its way, as rigorous as more traditional research methods.

Kathy remembers how ambiguity "feels" when she describes preparing
her proposal.

> I wished someone would have told me how to write a pro-
> posal to do a qualitative study in a school district. I followed
> the guidelines dictated by the Graduate School and modeled
> my request on that of a colleague who did a case study in one
> school. I did not consider the uncertain nature of the project I
> was studying or the fact that the continuous process of evalu-
> ation and revision would affect the choice of participants I
> would want to interview. I did not include unknown possibil-
> ities when I wrote my proposal. It seemed fine at the time to
> me and to my committee members.

In a subsequent letter, she continues:

> I told you during one of our conversations that I would have
> welcomed guidance when writing my proposal and espe-
> cially with my request to do research in the school system. I
> wish I had been advised to make the proposals open-ended
> enough to allow for the changes that take place when doing
> a qualitative study. I would have liked to have interviewed
> more people as the study evolved.

> I never considered writing an amendment to the request
> that had been approved by the university and the school dis-
> trict. I wish now that I would have pursued that. I raised
> many more questions than I answered.

Paula shares Kathy's concern:

> I "walked" a careful line between keeping within the guide-
> lines of my proposal and being able to "move with the
> groove" so that I could change plans and tactics as needed. I
> didn't understand how much latitude I had or would be al-

lowed to use. If I moved too far from my proposal, would I have to get my committee's approval? Would I have to go to the Internal Review Board?

Ann did not face this problem and writes:

My committee did believe in some flexibility in the proposal—if you need to keep interviewing, go ahead, one said. I simultaneously worried that 30 persons were too many and not enough. I now think, having collected the data, that 30 is just right. I believe I've reached the saturation point in terms of findings that Bogdan and Biklen (1982) speak of.

Kathy raises an additional issue about the implications of an emergent design for the proposal.

I think uncertainty is characteristic of many of our studies. Headings and organizational structure often develop during the process of data collection and analysis.

I could not have written an outline of my case study when I defended my proposal that looked like the nine-chapter document that has resulted from my study. I do believe that decisions about the general format need to be established in advance: where the review of literature fits, if the methodology used is described in a separate chapter, whether discussion of the findings is ongoing or a separate part of the report.

QUESTIONS

7. Will you be able to anticipate the "results" of your study? Should you? Could a pilot study or preliminary hours in context enable you to refine your focus? Anticipate results? Would you do this before your proposal defense?

8. Is your proposal open-ended enough to enable changes in direction, additional data sources or the elimination of some foci? Will it be acceptable to presume change, or must the changes be approved? By whom?

9. Do you know, as Kathy asked earlier, "where the review of literature fits, if the methodology used is [to be] described in a separate chapter, whether discussion of the findings is ongoing or a separate part of the report?"

10. Do your course work, outside reading, and experience enable you to bring a sense of wholeness to your proposal? What else do you need that might help you? That might help your committee?

11. Have you examined successfully defended qualitative theses for support in the areas of method and analyses?

The Literature Review

The correspondents refer to the literature review frequently. Although this topic is not isolated to the discussion of proposals, thinking about it early on may have some value.

Kathryn writes:

> For a qualitative study I have a lengthy review of the literature. The purpose was to describe why this study needed to be done, although there had already been a fair amount of research on the subject. I wanted to find the holes. The review also served to introduce support for the use of a theory to direct inquiry in a direction not used before ...; my interview guide was developed from coping theory. I wanted my committee to know that I knew about what had already been done, why I thought it did not adequately address the situation and why I was going to go about the study in the way I was about to describe.

Ann combines the review of the literature with the focus and significance of her study somewhat differently.

For the literature review in the proposal, 10 pages only seemed to be what everyone else had done and what my advisor wanted. I wanted my lit review to do more than set the stage for my study; I wanted it to be useful, definitive, up-to-date, and to be an entire chapter of my dissertation. My advisor didn't complain about this. I got the impression that if I wanted to do this amount of work, didn't get bogged down in it, and it didn't hold up the process of completion, then it was fine to go ahead.

Where does the literature review belong? One correspondent suggests:

A third decision, based on my major professor's preference was that I continuously review the literature throughout the study. Although I found doing this to be a lot of work, it was helpful. When one reads the literature and then notes what appears to be important, there is a good chance something is left out. In collecting the data and interpreting and analyzing it, I found that there was literature supporting some of my findings—literature which I had failed to include in the first drafts of the review.

In Pat's thesis, the literature "review is located throughout the dissertation. I only found the most appropriate literature descriptor *after* [italics added] the completion of the dissertation."

One of the issues hinted at in these selections is the struggle novice qualitative researchers have finding, reading, selecting, and incorporating the work of others. Who grants the authority to stop reading the literature? How does a novice qualitative researcher determine priorities when reading? What is the role of the literature review in the analysis of results? As it is described, the literature review often feels like a "separate activity" to the study; is it? How you reflect on and answer these questions will continue to inform your thinking and learning about qualitative research.

The Defense

The proposal defense is a topic several of the correspondents chose to recall. One correspondent, who wishes the following excerpt to remain unattributed, offers the following reflections about it:

I should mention that even though all of the committee members claimed they were open to a revised approach, at the proposal hearing two members of the committee seemed a little uncomfortable with the emergent nature of the analysis, in that they were, albeit in a speculative manner, trying to suggest general contexts for the study, such as historical comparisons. I may have to do a little bit of comparison ... to satisfy three of the members who suggested it. However, I feel confident I can convince them that the objective is to bring the material in selectively, to use it where it suits my purposes, rather than doing a comprehensive comparison (which I would like to do at a later time).

Dana, corresponding in 1998, shares a different experience:

I felt very fortunate to have not only strong and supportive guidance throughout the dissertation process but also a committee very supportive of qualitative research. For example, one professor encouraged me to think of Bill Moyers as a possible model for conversational interviewing rather than urging a strict and possibly unnatural interview protocol. At my proposal hearing, when I acknowledged that I could not predict my ultimate findings, a committee member told me, "Fry the fish you catch." From the beginning, I felt the committee's confidence in the process of qualitative research.

Robert found "that my chosen methodologies bore the most scrutiny from my committee at the proposal defense. They appeared satisfied with the research design once I convinced them of its rigor." Kathryn recalls, "It seemed that as long as I made my decisions and assumptions explicit, there were no questions asked by my committee. This was particularly true with sample size." Pat's committee "wanted to know if I could get permission from the school district and if I would manage the technical gathering of the data." (If you are interested in the subject of gaining entrée hinted at earlier, see the dissertation of Vonnie B. Taylor, a participant at the 1992 Qualitative Research in Education conference at the University of Georgia; at that time, she was a doctoral candidate from Texas A&M University. (Also see chap. 8 in Elliot Eisner's [1991] *The Enlightened Eye*.)

Ann credits her choice of committee members with the success of her proposal defense. Remember, too, that she had models of successful proposals to review.

> Given the feminist and qualitative awareness of my committee, no questioning occurred at the proposal defense about my use of the first person or my choice of conceptual framework. Ideas, concepts, and theories would basically emerge as I researched the question.

> In my proposal defense nothing was negotiated. My committee members (two of whom saw my proposal only in finished form) wanted to speed me on my way and focused on making my research methodology as clear as possible and on ensuring that my question was as clear and comprehensive as possible. In the methodology area, for instance, they wanted to know exactly how I would find the individuals for my a priori categories. They suggested further questions to ask.

> My interview, by the way, is an open-ended one, with set questions on areas or themes I want to cover. I follow Ives' (1980) advice in *The Tape Recorded Interview* (pp. 62–63).

Marie reports that her proposal defense also went well.

> It wasn't hard at all to get my study approved. I did what I wanted to, defended emergent designs carefully with well-placed quotes from the literature I alone was familiar with (at the time) but in which my committee was increasingly interested. When we discovered Judith Goetz, almost 2 years later, she was added to my committee in time for my defense; she bolstered the others' confidence in my approach.

Defense Questions

The question, "When is enough, enough?" reasserts itself in several variations.

The question of "how much literature review is enough?" or "When should I quit reviewing the literature?" was always on my mind. Even during the 2 weeks preceding my defense date, I wanted to review the literature on a particular topic because my third reader said I had ignored the literature in this area, even though the discussion of it only appeared in the final analysis. Also at the defense, I was told that I had "ignored" certain literature.… when is enough, enough???

Stuart provides a descriptive response to the question.

During the oral examination on my dissertation proposal (i.e., before I actually began fieldwork), one of my committee members asked an extremely important question: How will you know when you are finished? When do you know that you have collected enough data and can leave the field and begin writing? I think this was an excellent question, and I frequently use it with my own students today.

Quantitative researchers for the most part are able to state in advance when data collection will be completed. Based on the type of statistical analysis they want to do, they can project the sample size they need in order to generalize to the larger target population. Also, questionnaires are by their very nature fixed in time (there are just so many questions one can put into a survey). But when it comes to qualitative research, it is not always possible to know when one has collected enough data.

The answer I gave the committee member, and the answer I work with my students on today, is the following: When I begin this study, I have a set of concerns about patient selection and placement in nursing homes, and the communicational consequences of particular selection and placement decisions. But this set of concerns derives from a theoretical literature (the literature on social recruitment) and does not necessarily reflect issues that are of relevance to the groups I will be studying. (In other words, I am starting with an etic question right now, and hope to understand its emic significance for the particular groups I'll be working and studying with). During the course of the ethnographic fieldwork, my initial questions will be transformed into ones that are derived from, and that are related to, the experiences of the people I am studying. Instead of coming from an abstract, general theory of social recruitment, I will be asking questions about the categories of patients that each nursing home actually, in reality, in itself recognizes and does something about in terms of finding an available bed, making a roommate decision, etc., etc. So, I am hoping that the a priori questions with which I enter the field will be transformed into community-specific questions. Moreover, I wish to collect ample data to be able to leave the field when my original questions have been superceded by these community-relevant questions, and when I have collected both observational and interview data to answer these new questions.

Stuart's letter describes how the original focusing questions may become irrelevant to the actual study as it progresses. Because I was also educated about the etic–emic distinction, and because I believe qualitative research is more than a set of methods by which to get "results," I wrote Stuart and asked if he would be willing to write a little more on the topic for those who may not be familiar with it. He agreed.

I am surprised that I was the only person to mention the etic–emic distinction; it is extremely important to me with regard to ethnographic methodology and would have thought it would be used by many of your correspondents. My dissertation advisor was and is an anthropologist, and although my degree is officially in communication, I consider myself to be an anthropologist of communication. My dissertation advisor instilled in me the importance of transforming basic observational (etic) data into categories that are culturally meaningful (emic data). Therefore, I'd have to say that the etic–emic distinction was a choice made by me but heavily influenced by my dissertation advisor.

Part of the dissertation was concerned with the meaning, value, and significance of being assigned to each of the different "wards" or "sections" in the two nursing homes. In other words, two wards might look identical (in terms of quality of furnishings, whether they were carpeted or covered with linoleum, type of art work on the walls) and yet function differently: One might be a prestige ward, in the sense that older, sicker, and less alert patients were not placed there for residence. Emic analysis asks the questions: Do two comparable units (in terms of their physical and sense-related properties) function identically? Do they have the same meaning or value for the members of the group? In each of the two main data chapters of the dissertation (each chapter represents an ethnographic description and social interaction analysis for one nursing home), there is therefore an analysis of the functional meaning of each of he wards or sections and a comparative analysis of the functional equivalence or nonequivalence of each of the wards vis-à-vis the others. (For more information, see Kenneth Pike, 1967, *Language in Relation to a Unified Theory of the Structure of Human Behavior*, The Hague, Netherlands: Mouton.)

SUMMARY

Knowledge of qualitative research methodologies varies across individuals; so, too, does respect for persons and paradigms. From my interaction with all of the correspondents' materials, it seems that the amount of guidance offered, the degree of latitude to "do your own thing" and whom to please are important questions for the doctoral student to consider. As one correspondent put it (although more than several other voices corroborated the gist), personal circumstances matter, too. "You should also know that I started graduate school at an advanced age, nearly 50 years old, full of fear and doubt. I was particularly terrified of [the content I chose to focus on]; that's where most of my emotional turmoil arose. I was also sick a great deal of the time."

Where do graduate students gain the confidence to do their work? How much knowledge should a committee member assume? What is the value at any institution of an original piece of research? That is, is the essential purpose of the dissertation to do original work? To demonstrate research skills in an applied setting? To pass muster of the committee? Is the answer "all of the above?" Do/will/should standards of rigor vary across purposes? Susan offers some "insights into the process":

- I had done the legwork early with the literature review in the proposal. That was a lifesaver.

- I decided that when I worked, I would work. When I left my office, I was done for the day. Of course I thought about it. How can you not? But I also gave my brain a rest by doing laundry, schmoozing over puppies, and tending to children. (Actually, my children were 16–22, so I really didn't have to tend much.)

- Writing a qualitative policy study was good for me because it was not so ethereal; it was a topic, something that was tangible, something I could ask about. That was an immense help to me. I had a purpose and direction in my study. I wanted to make a difference, make people aware of what was happening, because it was something that was (and still is) affecting each of the institutions I visited.

- It was equally exciting to write a piece that connected things that hadn't been connected before. Suddenly I was an expert in something that many administrators were struggling with. Hey, maybe I could get a job! (In fact, I did. I completed a postdoc in the Provost's Office working with accountability and accreditation.) Really, that was one of the biggest factors in researching this particular topic.

- My chair asked even before my proposal what I wanted to do when I finished. She made sure that I knew that so that I could do a dissertation that would allow me to achieve my goals for the future; that's a practical tip for any student: Not only must you be interested in the topic, make sure that it will propel you forward to a job, to more publications, to whatever.

Several additional questions below bring this chapter to a close.

QUESTIONS

12. What if your committee doesn't like how you propose to do your work? What's negotiable? Can you defend your choices methodologically?

13. What if, as a faculty member, you cannot condone your student's proposal? What's negotiable? Can you support your suggestions methodologically?

14. How open are you to suggestions?

15. Can you answer basic questions such as, data from whom? When is enough, enough? What types of data? How much data? Where and how to incorporate the data?

16. Are you able to evaluate suggestions in terms of ethical, methodological, and contextual "fit?" Where can you argue? Where can you compromise? Can you?

5

SUPPORTING UNDERSTANDING

Maximizing Resources

> My most ardent piece of advice is to seek out and sur-
> round yourself with people who trust and support the or-
> ganic and often ambiguous nature of what you are trying
> to do. I consider myself extremely fortunate in that my
> committee is made up of women who believe in taking
> risks when it comes to issues of social justice, something I
> admire and want to emulate in my research endeavors.
> They offer the encouragement and support for me to, as
> one member often says, "take risks from a position of
> strength." (Kelly)

The first three chapters of this book include many conceptions of support
when undertaking qualitative research for the doctoral dissertation. Committee members, chairs, and advisors have helped their students throughout
the experience. Faculty members from other institutions have made their
services available to novice researchers and faculty members less familiar
with alternative methodologies. The annual Qualitative Research in Education Conference sponsored by the School of Education at the University of
Georgia is a third means by which doctoral students and faculty members
can find support. To address this important topic more thoroughly, this
chapter begins by providing references to the books and authors the correspondents found useful while contemplating and doing their studies. Because I include this information within the text of their letters, the
appearance of the references is neither alphabetical, categorical, nor exhaustive of all books available. Additionally, because I believe it may be
useful to have this information in context, and in order to save you from
searching the bibliography in the back for each individual text, I conclude
this chapter with the full citations of each of the books the correspondents

mention. The bibliography section at the back of the book, therefore, contains only the material that is either directly cited elsewhere or which directly influenced the writing of this book. Although reviewers suggested I "update the bibliography," I have found more than several useful websites, numerous recently published books and a plethora of chapters and articles about qualitative research that can easily be obtained. Additional resources include publishers' flyers for new books, qualitative research course syllabi, and bibliographies of completed dissertations. Most of the books mentioned herein have stood the test of time.

In addition to texts, more than several knowledgeable individuals are identified here as excellent resources. Formal study groups as well as less formal relationships including friends, family, and other faculty members also support the doctoral research process. Finally, I choose to conclude this chapter by highlighting the concept of time and the issue of money as supporting (or thwarting!) qualitative doctoral studies.

BOOKS

Ann mentions several books that helped her prepare for the proposal defense:

> At the beginning, but not during the writing, I found books such as Yin's (1984) helpful. It was too prescriptive later when I was well away into creating my proposal. After I finished my proposal and before the defense I found Marshall and Rossman (1989), Patton (1990), Bogdan and Biklen (1982), Sternberg (1981), and Ives (1980) helpful in tightening certain sections (methodology and analysis) and preparing for the defense of the proposal.

> A book I admire for its readability and entertainment value in what both the researchers say and the interviewed say (long quotes) is Aisenberg and Harrington's (1988) *Women of Academe: Outsiders in the Sacred Grove.*

Many correspondents also mention another text, Glaser and Strauss's (1967) volume, *The Discovery of Grounded Theory.* Additionally, my anonymous correspondent did some thinking about examples of qualitative research and writes the following:

> The most qualitative case study I know of in social science is Carlos Castandeda's research on Don Juan, resulting in his controversial dissertation. My dissertation is not nearly as qualitative and subjective. On the other hand, it is far from quantitative.... I do refer to the case study method, which I used as inspired by Mitchell (1983).

Kathryn writes that she "found LeCompte (1982) useful to anticipate issues from quantitatively trained researchers and tried to make explicit a number of decisions about the research." Gretchen remembers that she

> included the table from Guba and Lincoln (1981, p. 104) in my discussion of rigor and validity; I also quoted from pages where they discuss threats to validity. The issue of reliability was of most concern to the part of the study dealing with coding decisions, and I dealt with that using Holsti's composite reliability formula (1968, p. 137). My committee was satisfied; some journal reviewers have been critical of this formula.

Nancy writes that she

> swallowed the assumptions underlying the naturalistic paradigm hook, line, and sinker. I also looked to Lincoln and Guba (1985) regarding trustworthiness criteria, attempting, as they suggest, to triangulate data from different sources (interviews, observations, archival records, student transcripts, etc.). *Naturalistic Inquiry* was my dissertation project bible.

Jean also referred to Lincoln and Guba (1985).

> I used Lincoln and Guba's text, *Naturalistic Inquiry*, when taking my first qualitative research class and turned to it throughout my work on my dissertation. The clearly de-

fined processes were invaluable. I wish more people who conduct qualitative research would use the protocols they suggest. I am aghast at the number of professors and teachers conducting research in the Chicago area who do not get permission from parents and children before using their work or are even aware that that should be a consideration. When I mention anonymity and confidentiality, they act as though these are words whose meanings are foreign to them. I can't help but wonder WHO taught them to do qualitative research.... Mishler (1986), Carini (1979) and Duckworth (1987) were each tremendously helpful.

Marie, who successfully defended her thesis in 1982, recalls, "the most helpful single book I read was Schatzman and Strauss (1973)." Pat, who defended her thesis 8 years later, also found the Schatzman and Strauss book useful. Additionally, Robert suggested that Spradley (1980) and Taylor and Bogdan (1984) are useful texts for qualitative researchers. Mary K. refers to books from a different set of authors:

My research is further informed and strengthened by the scholarship of prolific African American women writers and critical thinkers such as Patricia Hill Collins, bell hooks, Audre Lourde, Toni Morrison—whose works have penetrated barriers and transgressed artificial limits that have been repeatedly placed in their paths.

Marilyn suggests several additional volumes that may be useful:

A book—Jan Zwicky's (1992) *Lyric Philosophy*—was invaluable. As I read it, all sense of how books had to be constructed, read, interpreted, was put on hold for long enough to allow a re-imagining of text and argument. But it came—and so, was made more powerful—after I had read feminist sociology and philosophy, after I had read about the importance of stories and narrative. It came after I was introduced to the legal storytelling movement—so much powerful research and writing there.

A brief review of this book might clarify Marilyn's enthusiasm.

> Two parallel texts, on facing pages, run through this unique volume. The left-hand text is Zwicky's exploration of the definition of a work as "philosophy," and a discussion of the notion of lyric. The right-hand text is "a scrapbook" of quotes from other authors, snippets of musical text, poems, and a handful of black-and-white photos. She presents the whole as "a new sort of overview" of the work of Wittgenstein, and an inquiry into Freud's concept of "primary process." [Annotation copyright Book News, Inc. Portland, Or. From Book News, Inc. May 1, 1993.]

> Zwicky, J. (1992). *Lyric philosophy.* Toronto Studies In Philosophy. Toronto, Ontario, Canada: University of Toronto Press.

Marilyn continues:

> The work of Richard Delgado is a good place to start, but there are many others, including an article by Russell Hamilton (1993). It was my standard, for he recognized the necessity of risk taking, and the fact that feminist research often involves much risk.

> Delgado, R. (1996). *The coming race war?* New York: New York University Press.

> Hamilton, R. (1993). On the way to the professoriate: The dissertation. *New Directions in Teaching and Learning, 54,* 47–56.

Kim offers some references linking methodology and music:

> Bamberger, J. (1991). *The mind behind the musical ear. How children develop musical intelligence.* Cambridge, MA: Harvard University Press.

Bresler, L. (1996). Basic and applied qualitative research in music education. *Research Studies in Music Education, 6,* 5–15.

Bresler, L., & Stake, R. E. (1992). Qualitative research methodology in music education. In R. Colwell (Ed.), *Handbook of research on music teaching and learning* (pp. 75–90). New York: Schirmer Books.

DeLorenzo, L. C. (1987). An exploratory study of sixth-grade students' creative music problem solving processes in the general music class. *Dissertation Abstracts International. 48*(07), 1689A. (University Microfilms No. 87-21099).

Hickey, M. (1995). *Qualitative and quantitative relationships between children's creative musical thinking processes and products.* Unpublished doctoral dissertation, Northwestern University.

Levi, R. (1991). *A field investigation of the composing processes used by second grade children creating original language and music pieces.* Unpublished doctoral dissertation, Case Western Reserve University.

Wiggins, J. H. (1992). *The nature of children's musical learning in the context of a music classroom.* Unpublished doctoral dissertation, University of Illinois at Urbana–Champaign.

Diana has a suggestion, too:

I modeled my interviews and use of abbreviated life histories on Etter-Lewis's work because of the emphasis she places on participants' words. As the Table of Contents from my dissertation illustrates, one chapter of the dissertation contains the first-person stories of the women I interviewed. Capturing their words and feelings was the primary goal of my work, and I believe using Etter-Lewis's methodology helped me to do so.

Etter-Lewis, G. (1993). *My soul is my own: Oral narratives of African American women in the professions.* New York: Routledge.

Barbara writes that she has "been greatly influenced by the philosophies of

postmodern and poststructural writings, including the writings of Judith Butler, Ann Garry, Marilyn Pearsall, bell hooks, Allison Weir, Alison Assiter. Feminist literary critique is just too restrictive for me. See:

Weir, A. (1996). *Sacrificial logics: Feminist theory and the critique of identity.* New York: Routledge.

I asked Chris, who writes about metaphor, "imaginal interaction," and openings in stories, to provide the citations for several of the works mentioned in his dissertation (chapter 3):

Brodkey, L. (1987a). Writing ethnographical narratives. *Written Communications, 4,* 25–50.

Brodkey, L. (1987b). Writing critical ethnographical narratives. *Anthropology and Education Quarterly, 18,* 67–77.

DeCastell, S., & Walker, T. (1991). Identity, metamorphosis, and ethnographic research: What kind of story is "Ways with Words?" *Anthropology and Education Quarterly, 22,* 3–22.

Duncan, G. (1996). Space, place and the problematic of race: Black adolescent discourse as mediated action. *Journal of Negro Education, 65,* 133–150.

Ellison, R. (1990). *Invisible man.* New York: Vintage. (Original work published 1947)

Greene, M. (1992). The passion of pluralism: Multiculturalism and the expanding community. *Journal of Negro Education, 61,* 250–261.

Greene, M. (1995). *Releasing the imagination: Essays on education, the arts, and social change.* San Francisco: Jossey-Bass.

Heath, S. B. (1983). *Ways with words: Language, life, and work in communities and classrooms.* New York: Cambridge University Press.

Heller, C. (1997). *Until we are strong together: Women writers in the Tenderloin.* New York: Teachers College Press.

The writing of McCarthy, C. (1992, 1993, 1995, 1998).

Morson, G. S. (1996). *Narrative and freedom: The shadow of time.* New Haven, CT: Yale University Press.

Tillich, P. (1957). *Dynamics of faith.* New York: Harper.

AUTHORS

Carol was fortunate enough to have a "dual" resource base, a book and its author! "My committee included Sherman Stanage, PhD, who is solidly in the camp of doing qualitative research. His book (1987) helped, as did discussions with him and the rest of my committee." Nancy Zeller and I studied with Egon Guba, and Marie Nelson worked with Judith Priessle (Goetz). Janice Ross and Dana Haight Cattani were students of Elliot Eisner. Both Kelly Clark Keefe and Katie Furney studied with Corinne Glesne. Chris Worthman worked with Chris Pappas. Additional kudos for more fine advisors appear throughout this book.

Several other correspondents, including Jean Stevenson and Pat Garlikov, had similar interactions with individuals highly regarded in the field of qualitative research. Experts are a valuable resource to novice qualitative researchers; committee members can also be role models. As Marilyn writes:

> My dissertation was, in many ways, a collaboration of the group, nurtured by my advisor's commitment to political activism, allowed to expand in its own way as I "became" a PhD. Risk seeps daily into my life as an administrator, and I am grateful, daily, for the loving apprenticeship of my dissertation.

QUESTIONS

1. What books are available to you? Have you searched in disciplines other than your own? Might faculty members in other departments be resources? Might your peers? Course work?
2. Are there any qualitative research experts in your department? On campus? At nearby universities? Available via the Internet?

OTHERS

Perhaps nothing has been less clearly written about but remains most crucial to the experience of doing qualitative research than the aspect of relationships. Student–committee interactions were discussed in chapter 3, but there are additional relationships forged, maintained, or broken during the dissertation process. I begin this section with the formal relationships particularly established to support the process and end up with those that are more personal.

Jean remembered one person whose attitudes and influence can directly promote an environment conducive to qualitative research. She writes, "The Dean when I began my studies was very inclusive in his acceptance of all forms of research. The current Dean continues to support that philosophical bent."

Study Groups

The majority of correspondents for this book continue to encourage participation in study groups. Maria remembers:

> My advisor had not been satisfied with the quality of her
> own dissertation and had been considering ways in which
> she might help her own advisees do more credible studies.
> She also believes that the dissertation should not be a
> meaningless academic exercise, but a substantive first step
> in establishing a student's professional research agenda
> and helping him or her to become part of a scholarly com-
> munity. Her own thinking about the links between theory
> and practice had been evolving, and she had been finding
> ways to theorize from practice-based data. The piece that
> was missing for her was the epistemological framework for
> defending "nontraditional" dissertations. By the late
> 1970s, she was ready to figure out the missing piece. At the
> same time, four of her doctoral students had reached the
> proposal stage, and she suggested the idea of forming a dis-
> sertation study group. We all agreed (taking it on faith that
> this would be a good idea and help us with the dissertation).
> She made it very clear that she did not have answers, and
> that we would be seeking answers together. Although all of
> us view her as our teacher and mentor, we also see her as a
> fellow learner and explorer. The collegiality that evolved
> among all of us was one of the most gratifying outcomes of
> the Study Group....
>
> I was the first member of the Study Group to begin working
> on my proposal and to take it to committee. My three peers
> were also working on theirs at the same time. We were so
> close together in the process I tend to think of us as going
> through it simultaneously. We learned from each other,
> from our experiences and encounters with committee
> members, from the references we were finding, and from

the ways in which we struggled with the epistemological underpinnings of our research....

We were not alone; we were not fighting epistemological battles by ourselves; we became, in a sense, our own community of scholars; we were a critical mass that could not be ignored or discounted as "flakes" who just wanted to do "quick and dirty" qualitative studies....

As we gained experience, we began to see that each study had a structure unique to its purpose, process, and results. The final dissertation documents did not follow the routine formula. They had an integrity of structure that emerged from the process and best communicated the results of the inquiry.

One of the consistent pieces of feedback we have received from faculty is that the documents are extremely readable and that the writing has a vitality to it. I believe that these qualities resulted, at least in part, from the fact that we could not follow a cut-and-dried formula and do justice to the knowledge generated through our research and the richness of our data.

Others correspondents also found value in study groups. Jean recalls:

Some of the faculty and graduate students met once a week for the Naturalistic Inquiry Seminar. It was a noncredit seminar, which served as a forum for sharing books, research, and ideas. I MISS IT. There was also an informal group of faculty and (usually doctoral) graduate students who met as a writing support group. I MISS THAT GROUP, TOO. We graduate students would meet formally at least once a month for lunch to talk, share current research, and fret. We also met for lunch, coffee, etc. much more frequently. We were a relatively "tight" group; membership changed as students graduated and moved on or began their research. The faculty encouraged our meeting together. It was through this group that I got the name of my typist.

Tim also recommends forming a study group.

> You are not alone. Seek out the advice and sympathetic ears of your colleagues. We have an organized group of graduate students who share problems, ideas, and bland cafeteria food. I have thought that it might be a good idea to get to know some of the qualitative-oriented students in other fields here at the university in order to share concerns about qualitative research. (Being qualitatively oriented, we would seek out better food.) I have met a lot of students at the University of Georgia's January conferences on qualitative research, so I do not feel I am alone as far as qualitative research goes.

I find Barbara's candor refreshing. At the time of this letter she was still a student:

> I do belong to a doctoral group that meets once a month in the home of one of our professors. This has been a significant factor in my doctoral experience, as a support group—in a private setting away from academia....

> I find the group to be tremendously helpful and supportive, simply because there is no other place that a doctoral student can sit and speak about their work. (No one else is the least bit interested, but I'm sure you already know that!) As for the content of the meeting, it's almost irrelevant to me. I learn by doing, not by listening, so if it were about collecting data, for example, it is meaningless to me unless I'm actually in the process of collecting data myself. I go for the social interaction with people who just "get it" in terms of the struggle we endure; juggling school, work, parenting, and even a social life at times!

QUESTIONS

3. What are the possibilities of forming a study group? Is there already one around inquiry issues in your—or another—department?
4. Might you enjoy a study group? Do you know of any faculty members who might be interested?

Respondents

Another perspective on personal support comes from two correspondents who explicitly mentioned that their research respondents were supportive of their efforts. Paula, who studied the power communication skills of female college presidents, recalls:

> Judith, you specifically asked me about the reaction and support from the participants. Some of their comments are in the methodology section, which is enclosed. I kept their comments in a notebook and took notes as I spoke with each during the initial telephone interview. The support from each with whom I spoke with was great (whether they were able to participate or not)! One called the study provocative. Some encouraged me to develop a training program after I completed. Nearly all were friendly, easy to talk to, and had ideas and comments of their own regarding the study. One told me that people were rarely interested in what she did; she thought that most women in her position would find it a "rare pleasure" to have me spend a week with them. I have more of these types of comments if you need them.

Jean also speaks highly of her two research participants:

> The two writers I selected were incredible! Not only had they donated their papers—an exposure of self that can't be imagined—but they were also willing to answer all sorts of questions from me.... I sent written questions to each of

them and also had an opportunity to interview both of them. The questions I asked were idiosyncratic. I did not have a list I asked both writers.

Family, Friends, New Colleagues

Family is an important support relationship. Barbara reflects: "Everything is *very* connected in my mind; paid work, parenting, teaching, research, play. It's all for the same ultimate goal: to live well, which is to enjoy one's life, to maintain a high quality of life (not necessarily, if at all, measured in financial terms)." Pam directly mentions her family: "I left at home each day a husband and three children (in 1993 they were 3, 6 and 19). My spouse was, and still is, very supportive." All of Jean's letters were laced with comments about family, making explicit a warm and intimate connection. Susan's letter in chapter 1 has a similar feel.

In the first edition, I mentioned that while I was a doctoral student, I heard stories about how some relationships break up because of the intensity and single-mindedness of the dissertation experience. I remember how focused I was, how little time I seemed to have—or perhaps chose to make—for anything or anyone else. Jim reflected on this theme for the second edition.

> Part of my dime-store psychology lesson is that an individual had better have a very understanding spouse if he or she is thinking of finishing in 4 years or so.... One powerful reason is that graduate school can fill a need not met at home. What better place to find that you have worth, that your views have an audience, that outsiders and others like you validate your existence, that you are someone. I bet there is a great statistical study in my target population and the rate of broken marriages among them—either before and during the time they were involved or just after they finished.... Graduate school allows for excitement, for the individual to shape, to control his or her destiny....

> On a few occasions [several friends] have spoken of what it's like to put yourself in the position of having strangers pass [judgment] on the merit of what you do—that is, to

pass on the merit of what is the essence of your existence.
They have agreed that it is not unlike standing naked in the
front window of Bloomingdale's at high noon. That kind of
excitement, along with the absolute vulnerability that goes
with it, that kind of rush—at least for me—is part of the lure
of graduate school at the doctoral level....

The sad thing is that the more of it you get, the more challenges you put in front of yourself and the more
time-consuming and complex you make it as you move
along, the more you isolate yourself from the very people
who supported your effort in the first place. Like combat,
you just don't know what it's like until you've been there.
And it is impossible to explain to others the consuming passion the Holy Grail can be. A tad melodramatic, I admit.
But I think I'm right.

I wonder who supports the <u>families</u> of focused qualitative researchers?
For how long must families be supportive? During the dissertation experience, the challenge seems to be in finding the time to do anything (or everything!) well, to care for oneself and others with conscious attention.

Several correspondents, including Jane, share the benefits of talking
with their friends as they work through their first qualitative research experience:

I've gotten into data analysis, and some pieces of the puzzle
are beginning to fall into place. I have found it very helpful
to talk to Cindy periodically; she is also doing a qualitative
study. We are attending different universities, are in different degree programs (hers is a PhD in nursing; mine an
EdD) and we have different designs (hers is ethnographic
and only uses interviews; mine is a case study and uses several forms of data). However, when we get together, we re-
assure one another, clarify, and give fresh perspectives.
Also, we aren't as judgmental as a professor might be, so
we can say anything! That support has been really valuable
for both of us.

I've noticed some emotional swings of doing this project. Cindy has too. I don't know how much is just part of doing a dissertation and how much is amplified by doing a qualitative study. We both have said how "stupid" we feel when we get frustrated. Sometimes I think, "This is so easy; I'm really on a roll." Other times I think I have nothing and its's all garbage. Cindy also reports similar feelings....

When I told my advisor about the new friend I've made (Cindy), she agreed that having someone to talk to WHO UNDERSTANDS QUALITATIVE RESEARCH is really valuable. Cindy and I have continued to benefit from brainstorming together and reassuring each other.

A part of friendship is feedback. A paragraph from Susan's letter (chap. 1) bears repeating:

I had (have) three friends who listened, helped me focus, and encouraged me endlessly through the process. The original model in the proposal simply would not work, so one friend made me talk out all of my data so that she could understand what I saw and heard. Then she made me talk out how I visualized how it all fit together. She pushed me to think! I wound up reorganizing my chapters to a more logical flow and using a theoretical framework that I know about but hadn't considered. The second friend simply said, "Just start." He encouraged me to take the three chapters from my proposal and put them in the correct format. Just keep at it. No excuses, just start. He wouldn't hear anything else. The third friend, my neighbor, walked with me every night. She helped with my physical health. Coupled with the fact that I had an office (away from home) where I could shut the door and concentrate; no classes to take, none to teach, nothing but writing.

Katie recalls:

I felt so grateful for the feedback I received from my professor of qualitative research and my classmates. This feedback was focused primarily on one chapter, but the advice and support I received helped me throughout. I tried to keep their words and thoughts on my mind as I wrote. This allowed me to have an audience to write to, as well as a set of guiding principles that helped me find new solutions to various writing challenges. Looking back, I can see that the people who helped me most were people that I trusted, respected, and admired in some way. Some (e.g., a favorite high school teacher) were present in my thinking frequently, yet had no idea that they were providing me with valuable "feedback."

QUESTIONS

5. Do your friends and family know the level of mental and emotional energy "handling ambiguity" requires?
6. Do you know by now that you CAN do this, with confidence, support and grace? Do you know you are not alone?

TIME AND MONEY

There are still other struggles and trade-offs facing novice qualitative researchers that have not been clearly or fully articulated, even here. The need for and pressures of time and money are described in a variety of ways. For example, Gretchen offers an example of the kind of juggling act that can occur:

I did my graduate work, one course at a time, while teaching high school French and Spanish full time. I used a sabbatical from high school to complete my on-campus residency requirement. As a 46-year-old student beginning PhD work in a new field, I had planned to take the full 7 years but finished in 5. There was a constant time crunch. Given a variety of other events beyond my control, my committee advanced the dates for several key milestones. My preliminary exam was moved ahead because my advisor was sure I was ready (even though I wanted several months more to review). I

passed all parts the first time, so I can't complain, but it was
very stressful to do it that way. Then, I was going to spend
the summer analyzing my pilot study and preparing to defend the proposal; when I came back June 8 from taking 45
high school Spanish students to Mexico, I found out that one
of my committee members was moving away in 2 weeks!
The committee told me to crank out the 75-page proposal
immediately, and they approved it June 18. A year later, they
put pressure on me to finish everything by late October in order to meet deadlines for November graduation. I think this
was because they wanted to nominate my dissertation for a
national award and the following year there would be two
others from the department that looked as if they had
award-winning potential. (My dissertation was among the
top eight nationally for the 1986 Redding Award, but didn't
make the final cut).

One correspondent describes another resource that was simultaneously a
constraint on the dissertation effort.

My dissertation was odd, because I used the facilities of another institution to complete it.… I would travel down to the
city, stay with friends for 2 to 3 days, and work there.… Originally, I had asked the curator of the collection (a PhD, who,
by the way, along with her staff, was wonderful to me) to
serve on my committee, but the then Dean of the Graduate
School began throwing up roadblocks. I was given the dis-
tinct impression that a dissertation done at "our" university
should have only "our" university faculty on its committee.

Several correspondents have reflected on the issue of distance—from
advisors, libraries, the university itself—as a benefit and drawback of their
experience. For example, several correspondents wrote that either their major advisor or another important committee member died while they were in
process. Human resources are fragile. Individual priorities differ. Stress is a
reality.

The human connection, even to issues of time and money, is also always
there. Jean writes: "I did receive a year-long scholarship that made life eas-

ier. Otherwise, my husband and I financed my work. I was an instructor for three semesters and supervised student teachers, which helped." In a postscript to her original letter, Paula adds, "I forgot to mention the size of my dissertation—215 pages … much too large and too expensive to have typed and duplicated. It cost over $750 for typing, editing, and duplicating—and I had very few mistakes (or it would have cost much more!) Will you address this issue?" Paula's dissertation is actually quite small compared with some (Stuart's = 500 pages, Jean's = 415 pages, Jane's = 390) and comparable with others (Nancy's = 230 pages, or mine = 282). The cost of production is worth investigating and considering when planning to undertake qualitative research for the dissertation. There are other supports and costs as well.

> I was also helped through the maze of institutional barbed wire by my typist. A longtime, respected graduate school typist, she was able to "catch" and question things which were almost clear. She was also a "walking style manual." However, the outside reader was poor. She editorialized and questioned the inclusion of items suggested by my committee. Her constant markings in what I presumed to be the final text required a total rerun of my dissertation and an additional $50.

QUESTIONS

7. What is your time schedule? Is it flexible? What is your "life load" like—that is, what other responsibilities also demand your time, your mental and emotional energy? Whose schedule are you on? Qualitative studies take longer than quantitative ones; can you "cut yourself some slack" once in a while and not feel guilty? Do you remember the word FUN???

8. Are any of the faculty members with whom you are working planning sabbaticals in the near future? Retirement? Professional moves? Is your timetable compatible? Can it be adjusted? What are the tradeoffs? Are they worth it?

9. What are the costs of this effort in strictly financial terms? Are there departmental scholarships available for the dis-

sertation year? Is there travel support if you choose to give a presentation about your work, or, are you working full-time? What is realistic for you? What can you afford?

10. How much are you really on your own? How willing are you to enlist the support of others? Can you "be nice" to yourself and still feel you are making progress?

11. Can you type?

SUMMARY

Much more could be written about the nature and value of dissertation support systems; as a theme it runs throughout this book. Support may come from external resources or internal goals, from the university or a child. If it is not clear to you yet, support is a necessary quality of the qualitative dissertation. As one correspondent recalls:

> The qualitative process takes a tremendous amount of patience. I'm sure more than one kind and wise soul told me this, but it has only been from doing that I now realize it. Qualitative inquiry and the growth that occurs *while engaging in it takes three times the time you initially think it will, more energy than many humans expend in their entire lifetime, and a lot of nerve.* [italics added]

The stories of Marie and Stuart enable us to view contemporary possibilities and constraints from a historical perspective:

> Dear Judy,   November 9, 1990
>
> I've been wondering where I put your letters for weeks, but today, having set aside a whole day for housecleaning, I found them. Given the constant state of pressure and denial (smile) I experience, let me respond now before I lose them again.... Advance copies of my new book, *At the Point of Need: Teaching Basic and ESL Writers*, which is hot off the press, arrived today from Boynton/Cook. (It's a perfect example of the negotiations—or more precisely, the sacri-

fices—faculty as well as graduate students have to make to do the kind of research we do.) Since I'm between deadlines right now, let me begin.

My case may be different from those of some people you study, for I had very few negotiations to make during the process of my dissertation. That does not mean I always did what I wanted to, however. When I was first in my doctoral program, quantitative research was all that I was taught, and in 1970 I left Georgia A.B.D. (all but dissertation) because I could not find a dissertation topic I was willing to devote a year of my life to doing. At that point I had taken at least 20 quarter hours in research design and statistics, courses I found to be extremely interesting and intellectually stimulating. It was the topics of studies that could be done using those methods that were neither interesting nor stimulating to me.

When I returned 8 years later, I had to revalidate my course work, retake my comprehensive exam, and retake the final course in the research sequence which was still entirely quantitative. In my department, however, interest in case study research had been aroused by the work of Janet Emig and Don Graves, but I did not want to do case studies. I wanted to study the classrooms of writers who teach writing; I had no idea how I would go about selecting them, for I had known many writers who taught quite traditionally, disregarding entirely what they told me about how they themselves wrote.

Although Judith Goetz (who with Marki LeCompte was working on an important book on qualitative research in education) was already at my institution, my male mentors did not know her then and did not know she was teaching a course in qualitative methods in the Social Science Education department. I was entirely on my own when it came to preparing myself methodologically. I read and read and read, dozens of articles and books, until, finally, after about 3 months of following blind alleys—I had never heard the term ethnography—I discovered Schatzman and Strauss (1973) and a number of anthropological methodologists. The night I found Schatzman and Strauss I stayed up all night reading. In symbolic interactionism I knew I had found what I needed for my study.

Stuart, who—while on sabbatical leave in Australia—was responding to a question I had about his Table of Contents (see Appendix B), also enables us to appreciate the changing times.

You asked about the NOTES section at the end of each chapter: I don't have a copy of the dissertation here with me, so I cannot refer to the particular notes you are speaking of. Overall, I decided to create a notes section at the end of each chapter, rather than footnotes, because when I wrote the dissertation I used a typewriter and not a personal computer or word processor. As you can imagine, when I had to submit revised versions of chapters after they had been read and critiqued by my dissertation advisor, it was much easier doing a cut-and-paste job on pages of text without worrying about footnotes on the bottom. It seems hard to imagine today, but only 10 years ago people like me were working without benefit of personal computers, without any software that with a simple command can renumber footnotes, etc., etc. So, there was no requirement that dictated the use of endnotes; I just found it a much easier way of handling note material.

Although I was a grouch at the time I had to learn how to use the computer and word processing software in order to get the dissertation completed, after reading Stuart's account I have begun to treat my computer with slightly more regard. Its help in the completing of this 2nd edition has been even more valuable. Support doesn't have to be human. Even chocolate works!

REFERENCES FOR CHAPTER 5:

Aisenberg, N., & Harrington, M. (1988). *Women of academe: Outsiders in the sacred grove.* Amherst, MA: University of Massachusetts Press.

Bamberger, J. (1991). *The mind behind the musical ear: How children develop musical intelligence.* Cambridge, MA: Harvard University Press.

Bogdan, R., & Biklen, S. (1982). *Qualitative research for education: An introduction to theory and methods.* Needham Heights, MA: Allyn and Bacon.

Bresler, L. (1996). Basic and applied qualitative research in music education. *Research Studies in Music Education, 6,* 5–15.

Brodkey, L. (1987a). Writing ethnographical narratives. *Written Communications, 4,* 25–50.

Brodkey, L. (1987b). Writing critical ethnographic narratives. *Anthropology & Education Quarterly, 18,* 67–77.

Carini, P. F. (1979). *The art of seeing and the visibility of the person.* Grand Forks, ND: North Dakota Study Group on Evaluation.

Colwell, R. (1992). (Ed.). *Handbook of research on music teaching and learning.* New York: Schirmer Books.

DeCastell, S., & Walker, T. (1991). Identity, metamorphosis, and ethnographic research: What kind of story is "Ways with Words?" *Anthropology and Education Quarterly, 22,* 3–22.

Delgado, R. (1996). *The coming race war?* New York: NYU Press.

DeLorenzo, L. C. (1987). An exploratory study of sixth-grade students' creative music problem solving processes in the general music class. *Dissertation Abstracts International, 48 (07),* 1689A. (University Microfilms No. 87-21099).

Duckworth, E. (1987). *"The Having of Wonderful Ideas" and other essays on teaching and learning.* New York: Teachers College Press.

Duncan, G. (1996). Space, place and the problematic of race: Black adolescent discourse as mediated action. *Journal of Negro Education, 65,* 133–150.

Ellison, R. (1947, 1990). *Invisible man.* New York: Vintage.

Etter-Lewis, G. (1993). *My soul is my own: Oral narratives of African American women in the professions.* New York: Routledge.

Glaser, B. G., & Strauss, L. (1967). *The discovery of grounded theory.* New York: Aldine de Gruyter.

Greene, M. (1992). The passion of pluralism: Multiculturalism and the expanding community. *Journal of Negro Education, 61,* 250–261.

Greene, M. (1995). *Releasing the imagination: Essays on education, the arts, and social change.* San Francisco: Jossey-Bass.

Guba, E. G., & Lincoln, Y. S. (1981). *Effective evaluation.* San Francisco: Jossey-Bass.

Hamilton, R. (1993). On the way to the professoriate: The dissertation. *New Directions in Teaching and Learning, 54,* 47–56.

Heath, S. B., (1983). *Ways with words: Language, life, and work in communities and classrooms.* New York: Cambridge University Press.

Heller, C. (1997). *Until we are strong together: Women writers in the Tenderloin.* New York: Teachers College Press.

Hickey, M. (1995). *Qualitative and quantitative relationships between children's creative musical thinking processes and products.* Unpublished doctoral dissertation, Northwestern University, Chicago.

Holstoi, O. R. (1968). *Content analysis for the social sciences.* Reading, MA: Addison-Wesley.

Ives, E. D. (1980). *The tape-recorded interview: A manual for field workers in folklore and oral history.* Knoxville, TN: University of Tennessee Press.

LeCompte, M. D., & Goetz, J. P. (1982). Problems of reliability in ethnographic research. *Review of Educational Research, 52,* 31–60.

Levi, R. (1991). *A field investigation of the composing processes used by second grade children creating original language and music pieces.* Unpublished doctoral dissertation, Case Western Reserve University.

Lincoln, Y. S., & Guba, E. G. (1985). *Naturalistic inquiry.* Beverly Hills, CA: Sage.

Marshall, C., & Rossman, G. (1989). *Designing qualitative research.* Beverly Hills, CA: Sage.

Mishler, E. G. (1986). *Research interviewing: Context and narrative.* Cambridge, MA: Harvard University Press.

Mitchell, C. J. (1983). Case and situational analysis. *Sociological Review, 31,* 187–211.

Morson, G. S., (1996). *Narrative and freedom: The shadow of time.* New Haven, CT: Yale University Press.

Patton, M. Q. (1990). *Qualitative evaluation and research methods.* Beverly Hills, CA: Sage.

Schatzman L., & Strauss, A. L. (1973). *Field research: Strategies for a natural sociology.* Englewood Cliffs, NJ: Prentice-Hall.

Spradley, J. P. (1980). *Participant observation.* New York: Holt, Rinehart & Winston.

Stanage, S. (1987). *Adult education and phenomenological research: New directions for theory, practice and research.* Malabar, FL: R. E. Krieger.

Sternberg, D. (1981). *How to complete and survive a doctoral dissertation.* New York: St. Martin's Press.

Taylor, S. J., & Bogdan, R. (1984). *Introduction to qualitative research methods.* New York: Wiley.

Tillich, P. (1957). *Dynamics of faith.* New York: Harper.

Weir, A. (1996). *Sacrificial logics: Feminist theory and the critique of identity.* New York: Routledge.

Wiggins, J. H. (1992). *The nature of children's musical learning in the context of a music classroom.* Unpublished doctoral dissertation, University of Illinois at Urbana-Champaign.

Yin, R. K. (1984). *Case study research: Design and methods.* Newbury Park, CA: Sage.

Zwicky, J. (1992). *Lyric philosophy.* Toronto Studies in Philosophy. Toronto: University of Toronto Press.

6

UNDERSTANDING
BY FOCUSING

Ownership, Autobiography, Ethics

> Know that you will (most likely) form a relationship with
> your topic. Like other relationships, this one has good and
> bad moments! As time goes on, you will increasingly hear
> your topic, see it, feel it, and talk about it (perhaps inces-
> santly). You may become distracted and/or bore others
> quickly, but you will grow to know and love (and sometimes
> hate) your study. (Katie)

Research texts often assume that the researcher has a problem to pursue.
Little time is spent discussing what is and is not a problem; more is spent
suggesting where to look for one (Meloy, 1989). Determining a focus in
qualitative research usually includes examining and reexamining the research context, changing one's mind and giving up preconceived notions of
what is important. Understanding the focus occurs nearer to the middle and
the end—as opposed to the beginning—of the inquiry. How an individual
finds focus and the focus that an individual finds are directly linked to who
the individual is. A focus may "emerge" from context, but it actually takes
shape as a result of how an individual looks at a given context, what is perceived, and what that individual determines to do with all of that "stuff." If a
statistical analogy may be used, finding focus is, in a sense, the result of an
"interaction effect" of person and context; and, like statistics for some, it's
not always easy to grasp. Lisa, early in her doctoral program in 1998,
writes: "As far as my own research interests go, I have so many that I've had
a difficult time narrowing them to a workable load."

FINDING FOCUS

Several correspondents reflect on how they found a focus, and what that focus means to them. Nancy writes:

> I knew I was interested in meta-inquiry and that I didn't want to do and report on an experimental project. I further knew that I wanted to write a dissertation that developed and provided convincing support for an argument rather than one that collected and tinkered with data until I found an argument the data would support. That statement contains a redundancy, but so few dissertations nowadays develop and support an argument that maybe it's worth repeating. I would guess that my background in speech (BS) and English (MA) had a lot to do with how my dissertation project was conceived and carried out.

Kathy recalls:

> Focus was a problem at the onset, that is, keeping focused on the questions that guide the study. Michael Patton helped at last year's Qualitative Research in Education Conference (School of Education, UGA) when he told me that it is all right to talk about the big picture, and that it is not necessary to look carefully at all of the happenings that pose interesting questions.

Kathryn explicitly links her thinking to the literature in her field; she notes how her understandings grew and changed.

> I started my doctoral education interested in the physiologic stress response and how to reduce stress for acute myocardial infarction (AMI) patients in the coronary care setting. Before I began course work in a new content area (stress and coping) I really believed that the problem was well understood and that it was simply a matter of going about creating the right set of experiments to find the "best" ways to reduce

stress for this group of patients. However, as I explored the general and specific stress literature and tried to apply it to clinical experiences, I began to recognize the limits of current understanding. Pieces were missing; what was described by authorities simply did not make sense…. I still quite clearly recall the quarter when I decided that too little was known about what was happening, or at least it was not documented, to begin to develop experiments. In other words, it was a qualitative not a quantitative problem. This was, I am sure you will understand, a very exciting and awesome process … changing worldviews and trying to integrate alternative research paradigms with those of an entire education in the sciences. I was, after all, a critical care nurse accustomed to measuring and quantifying. It was just that I was also coming to recognize that the problem I wanted answers to, that is, the best way to reduce stress for AMI patients was more complex than addressed in relevant literature; there was much unknown that I was just beginning to acknowledge. I now very honestly believe that we have delayed our development as a science because we have tried to approach all nursing and patient questions from the quantitative approach. We can change that, however. In a way this paralleled my frustration with the fact that, despite all my prior education, I had not as yet encountered a way to handle things such as observations and hunches.

OWNERSHIP

Correspondents contributing to the first edition wrote explicitly about "ownership" of the dissertation. One of the "feelings" about what it means to do qualitative research appears to be a strong, definite sense of direct, personal connection with the processes and product, in large part, I think, because of the connection of thinking and writing. Jean is just one of the correspondents whose letters suggested this topic.

Earlier in this letter, I mentioned choice and ownership and the roles both play in my own work. I believe that being al-

lowed to make choices concerning topic, etc. have a pro-
found effect on ownership and ultimately on the
development of a strong sense of responsibility for the
piece. In *Lessons from a Child: On the Teaching and
Learning of Writing*, Lucy McCormick Calkins (1983)
says "when children are makers of reading, they gain a
sense of ownership over their reading. As we've seen again
and again, owners are different from tenants" (p. 156).
Choice is the key. In writing process classrooms, the writers choose their own topics. No one tells them what to
write. The power choice gives the writer involved ownership and is "awesome" to behold; with that ownership comes responsibility.

Jean continues, mentioning ownership again as connected to the focus of
her study.

I threw objectivity out the window in the sense that one of
the criteria used in selecting the authors for the study was
that I liked their work and would use it. Kathy Gershman
gave me a very good bit of advice about selecting subjects—You MUST be willing to live with them for the rest
of your life.

The anonymous correspondent wrote: "I assumed the dissertation would
be worthwhile because the materials within it were interesting to me. My
interest had to carry me through many years, from proposal to completion,
which it did." For Marie, a sense of purpose and ownership of the topic were
crucial:

I had gone through the program once, in the late 60s, when
the field was not ready for me to do what I wanted to do. So,
I left school and did what was more meaningful to me.
When I went back, I found things had changed. My several
mentors were extremely supportive and open-minded. I
never felt that I was jumping through hoops to get a union

card (though if I'd stayed to finish the first time, I would have felt just that).

I think my more positive experience had something to do with the fact that I really didn't care much about having a PhD.... I was in school because it seemed that I could have more influence, could help more teachers and more kids, if I got the degree.

AUTOBIOGRAPHY

Correspondents for the second edition were even more direct in linking their studies to themselves, suggesting it is exactly who we are—our background experiences, knowledge, and understandings—that shapes our inquiry. Janice writes:

I began my doctoral program in education after a decade as a professional dance critic and several years as a dance historian. Coming to Education from these two humanistic practices, I was already familiar with historical and critical methods of writing and researching. *I realize now in retrospect* [italics added] that I assumed that whatever kind of dissertation I wrote would be qualitative, and that my experience as an arts critic and historian would inform what I did....

My task was made easier because my subject was one in which there had been little if any traditional research. After a literature review I began collecting data.... I was comfortably at home. I was behaving as a historian and critic would.

Marilyn, whose poem precedes chapter 1, dealt specifically with the concept of autobiography in her thesis. In a lengthy excerpt from her dissertation, she presents her argument:

Readers, I ask you to make a commitment here, to play this with me, to pretend that you have asked (if you have not asked) what it is that makes autobiography desirable, permissible, theoretically compelling in this dissertation. [I will try to answer your question]. Boldly: "Why autobiography?" ...

I have been interviewing women writing dissertations. It seems to me that the script needs to be rewritten....

What is it that autobiography allows in my dissertation? Why, in other words, is it necessary to this project? Three possibilities seem most immediately important. First, autobiography announces unambiguously the arrival of a woman subject—gendered, embodied, and located in ways directly related to the life experiences an autobiography can reveal—in the masculine world of academe. It allows, in other words, disruption. More specifically, my autobiography allows an exploration of the development of the varied voices I use as writer and scholar and demonstrates that I have "learned to write" (and thus to think) in ways directly related to my gendered, embodied, and located experiences. It accepts, to some extent, the male–female opposition. In demonstrating my own coming to writing, autobiography, like the inclusion of first names rather than just initials in citations, challenges the transparent maleness of the generic academic. It makes apparent those parts of my writing self that would be erased were I allowed only "academic writing" in the dissertation; it speaks, in other words, to the sort of academic I would become. In being consciously resistant to erasure of my "nonacademic" voices, it implies the question of erasure with regard to other—equally gendered, embodied, and located—writers of dissertations.

Second, the political, feminist standpoint from which I write has grown out of the same lived experiences that have nurtured my voice; autobiography reveals, more clearly it seems to me than I could argue in more disembodied ways, the historically located personal importance of this project.

It is not uncommon for women to be heavily, personally in-vested in their research [perhaps men as well, but they have not come to me with their stories]. Dissertations are not, in such cases, simply exercises, demonstrations that we are able to design and carry out research projects. It is not suffi-cient in such cases that we find just any question that has not been addressed or that we join in whatever ongoing project may be current in the lab; and we may refuse to put aside our concerns in favor of a more "doable" dissertation, feeling that the work we envision ourselves doing—or are already actually involved in—should not be put off until "after the dissertation." (A few examples suggest that this may be said generally of students who have strong connec-tions with oppressed cultural, ethnic, and/or class groups.) Sometimes, for instance, personal crisis instigates the work, as in the case of S, who set out to find a cure when her daughter was diagnosed with juvenile onset diabetes. Sometimes personal integrity places demands on the re-searcher that extend beyond the event of the dissertation: S promised the participants in her study that she'd share their stories with others by publishing scholarly articles. Some-times the need is only vaguely felt: S lamented, "even my advisor doesn't understand why my dissertation can't be just any dissertation." Students who bring these kinds of personal commitment to their research disrupt the ritual separations. They also bring with them their need to be sup-ported in this personally compelling research. This need seems to me to want recognition.

Third, in being identifiably (autobiographically) a woman's voice, this dissertation will, I hope, provide an alternative "mirror," an image suggested by Elspeth Probyn's (1993) discussion in *Sexing the Self* of the epistemological and on-tological moments that occur when women read other women's writing. I see it reflecting not some hypothesized lack but rather, and precisely because each reader brings her own autobiography to its reading, varied possibilities for change in the tenaciously dominant-culture culture of academe—a rewriting of the scripts.

One of Mary K.'s reflections fits in here, too.

I remember hearing bell hooks, in a speech at a feminist conference in Toledo in 1995. She spoke of the criticism that accompanies her work, some saying that much of what she writes is not academic. Her critics contend that's because her work speaks to the experiences of many people who are outside of the ivy covered wall of academe. She continued by referring to the number of times her works have been used by other prolific mainstream, white, male and female writers and thinkers, with no mention or credit given to her works or her insights. She then referred to a number of her fondest critics who "write her in to write her off," to point to her ideologies and then denigrate her or her works for a variety of reasons.

That evening, her words, especially "being written in to then be written off," hit a very deep nerve in my literary being. At that time, I didn't realize the depth to which those words would penetrate, but I have a constant reminder reflected in my own pursuit to complete this tedious process called the dissertation.

Kelly and Diana share Marilyn's passion for the power of autobiography. Kelly describes her work:

My inquiry involves developing a collective case study of six women academics that have experience being first-generation college students from working class or poor backgrounds.... In brief I was interested in exploring the women's narratives that described their formative background experiences, their journeys into and through higher education, and their sense of self in relationship to these events and life choices....

Even if I weren't what it is I am studying, which I am, the whole bloody thing would be subjective.... But then you knew that. I am from a working class background and have experience being the first-generation in my family to go to college. These life "attributes" and their relationship to my own identity development are, in essence, the roots of my inquiry. My gendered, classed, sexual, and ethnic sense of self has informed aspects of the direction my research has taken and, in turn, my sense of self has been informed by aspects of the research process. This inextricable link has been explored and embraced, and now I would never leave home to do research without it. Perhaps this is tangential—you likely allow for some of that, but my experience with all that I have mentioned (process, product, personal) could not have been as fully "realized" without the relationships I have developed along the way.

And Diana writes:

I admit that I was not an objective and detached observer and recorder throughout my dissertation process. I worried about this a great deal at the time and was amply warned by committee members and colleagues that it would be difficult to write a dissertation on a topic I was so very closely attached to; this was certainly true! I wanted to know from other women what it was like to be simultaneously a single mother, a social service recipient, and a postsecondary student. My interest was not so much (certainly not exclusively) with the logistics of managing children, school, social and family responsibilities, etc., but more so with how the women defined themselves given a very negative portrayal by society. Initially, my most basic question was "how do these women make sense of their lives as single mothers and students?" As I grappled with this question, I began to realize that it was a question I was also asking of myself and (rhetorically) of my own mother as well. It was a very personal and at times painful question. My feelings on the topic are still evolving, as reflected by the title of a journal article I recently completed based on this research: "Great Expectations: Single Mothers in Higher Education" (requested and in review for a proposed special issue of *Anthropology and Education Quarterly*). At least part of what I learned through my dissertation study is ... as true of myself as it was of the women I interviewed.

I wrote the following in the methodology chapter of my dissertation (it was, by the way, the most difficult chapter for me to write!):

> Personal and private lives are not distinct—we do not literally cross borders between them, but rather occupy both simultaneously. Who I am as a private individual does not simply influence who I am as a researcher, we are one and the same.... Personal and professional lives intersect in meaningful ways; thus, my interest in single motherhood is personal as well as professional. Like the women I interviewed, I too am a single mother and a student. In many ways, I am an insider whose experiences mirror those of the women I am studying. Thus, my story is intimately connected to the stories these women relate and to the composite story I have crafted from their narratives.... Like them, I am actively involved in constructing my own story of single motherhood and in making sense of experiences that both restrict and enhance who I am. (pp. 43–44)

That I was "allowed" to write this personally in my dissertation reflects, I think, the support of my committee and especially my chairperson.... More importantly, however, it provides a record—MY record—of what it is like to write about my own life in the context of other similar lives. From the distance of a few years, I firmly believe this to be its greatest value. Writing a dissertation is (at least in part) an academic experience in learning to do research; in my case, it was much more than that—it was an experience in learning important lessons about myself.

Mary K. concludes:

I think my words will reflect growth, strength, and certainly the passion that has been spearheading my drive to complete this degree, to share my words, and to tell the stories of those who have previously been without voice. [JUDY: sometimes that's the researcher him or herself; it's a story untold, too!]

Clearly, at the beginning of the 21st century, the question of "ownership" of one's thesis takes on additional meaning. Katie writes about the making of connections.

I've worked at the University since the fall of 1986. During most of that time, I have been employed through federally funded research and model demonstration projects, though over the years, I began to do increasingly more teaching and supervision in our graduate programs in special education and educational leadership. The projects with which I have been associated have included quantitative studies of the effects of specific curriculum interventions, a project focused on enhancing the process through which students with disabilities and their parents plan for the future, and policy studies of federal initiatives on school-to-work transitions and Vermont's Act 230. My dissertation grew out of the Act 230 study. It was a focused and directed topic, in that my mentor–advisor–boss strongly suggested that I do my dissertation on something closely related to work. On the other hand, it felt less directed than the topics of some of my doctoral cohort members, in that they seemed to be focused on lifelong and life-changing themes that were of great personal interest. The wonderful thing for me is that my topic became connected to things that I consider to be my life's work. *Perhaps that is part of the beauty of qualitative research for me—even a topic that seemed initially to be a bit distant became part of me, something that helped me to learn and change, something that ultimately became a defining theme and part of my focus in work and life in general.* [italics added]

As I reread Katie's thoughts, I am caught momentarily off-guard; I am surprised that more correspondents didn't write directly about the transforming nature of doing qualitative research for the dissertation. Two who did are Nancy and Tim. Nancy writes:

One thing I discovered about conducting case studies is that you can never anticipate the ways in which things can go wrong and that you'd better be prepared to undergo some kind of change as a result of doing the case study. I believe that a personal transformation in understanding that moves from logic–reason toward intuition–emotion is inevitable and, further, that the case researcher must be willing to see her or himself as a wrong thing in a right world in order to be transformed into the filter through which experience is shaped and given meaning. This transformation, which cannot be foreseen or planned for, may involve learning to view things in a simpler way than academics—even naturalists—are used to.

Tim adds: "<u>Commit yourself to your research</u>. Graduate school has evolved into the equivalent of the Shao-lin monastery for me in some respects. It has been a period of great intellectual and emotional growth, a transformation."

SUMMARY

Qualitative research is inexorably linked to the human being as researcher. I am curious to know whether quantitative researchers feel as possessive about their work as "my" correspondents and I do? If they do, what is the essence of that linkage—for example, person to topic? Person to results? Are any of our experiences of meaning making the same? Whatever might be the case, perhaps an excerpt from one of Jean's early letters offers a fitting closure here:

> Going through the doctoral process is not for the faint-hearted. You have to want it so badly that you can taste it. Having a sense of ownership of your learning and your research can certainly help you get through—sustain you—when the light at the end of the tunnel is red and the alternative tunnels seem blocked with debris.

As I reflect on Jean's comments, I am not sure <u>now</u> that in my past researches I have "owned" anything; rather, the context took hold of me and we danced. Even though I've left before the music was over, I still hum parts of the melody we shared, still remember the ambience of the scene. The lives of the individuals with whom I've interacted dance on, without me but also within me. Some of the learning I did there has claimed <u>me</u>. I would like to suggest, therefore, that the aphorism "good things never last" is wrong; perhaps good things—by which I mean the emerging sophistication of the researcher as a thinking, feeling, interactive human being who is the research instrument—will last. What we come to "own," then, is not the context but our responsibility to it and our emerging ability to handle it well.

QUESTIONS

1. What are the current influences on your thinking? Educational background, personal experiences, contemporary course work, faculty interests? How will you choose a focus? Can you identify areas of interest to you, ideas that might be fun to explore? What are you curious about?

2. Do you have any idea how you will sort out 'important' questions from unimportant ones? 'Big' ones from 'little' ones? How will you keep track of your ideas?

3. Have you considered what it means to be "the research instrument"? How do you view yourself in relationship to

your proposed focus and the people with whom you will work to investigate it? Who are you as a researcher? What do you expect from yourself and toward others?

4. Are you prepared to question yourself? Your motives? Your assumptions, values, and sense of priorities? How 'close' to yourself are you willing to become?

5. How much ambiguity are you willing—and able—to handle?

6. What is, or how will you define, the nature of your relationship with your research participants? Who is responsible for defining it?

7. Might a suggested trilogy of research "Rs" be respect, responsibility, and rigor? What might each imply about the ethics of the study? About your interactions within the focus and context of the study? Do you think about this?

ETHICS

Ethical issues arise in qualitative inquiry, some of which are anticipated and prepared for (e.g., anonymity and confidentiality), whereas others (e.g., observable violations of the law) often are not. Sharon provides a rich description of such circumstances; excerpts are offered here.

During the study, ethical dilemmas emerged that no one had anticipated. I uncovered and reported troubling data regarding … illegal practices…. [A] threatened lawsuit and the involvement of university attorneys jeopardized the research project and the completion of my degree….

My personal ethical frame is largely drawn from conservative Christian beliefs and biblical principles. The religious heritage of my church and family is central to my world's view. I use the Golden Rule as a principle of daily living.

In seeking a way to sort and articulate my priorities, I have found John Rawls's (1971) theory of justice to be key….

The flow of power and resources must benefit the least advantaged....

While negotiating permission to conduct the study, I relied on three established principles of fieldwork: informed consent, anonymity, and nonintervention.... We [my research subject and I] agreed my role would be observing and interpreting events as they naturally occurred. [He] indicated these were adequate safeguards and agreed to the study.

As I left ... I was relieved. I had passed muster. [He] was the gatekeeper....

I felt managed, dependent [on his 'OK']. I had permission ... but I knew [it] could be withdrawn at any time....

During initial negotiations, [he] did not ask nor did I consider inviting him to critique and approve drafts....

At the beginning of the study, it seemed unlikely that I could exploit [him]. He was at the apex of his career, I was a doctoral student....

From my earliest studies of qualitative methods with Louis Smith (1990), I had pondered the ethics of ethnography. I recognized the potential vulnerability of research subjects and was determined to avoid exploiting those I studied. James Agee's (1939) words haunted me:

> It seems to me curious, not to say obscene and thoroughly terrifying, that it could occur to an association of human beings ... to pry intimately into the lives of an undefended ... group of human beings for the purposes of parading the nakedness, disadvantage and humiliation of these lives before another group of human beings. (p. 7)

… The central ethical dilemma … began during the
second month of the study.…

I began to ask myself Becker's (1970) question:
"Whose side are you on?" When confronted with the
dissymmetry of power … I began to realize I must side
with the least advantaged … I wanted to intervene, …
but I stood by silently collecting data. I felt the frustration of conducting "inaction research" (Gentile,
1994), fiddling while Rome burned.

Early in the first year of the study, I decided it would no longer be ethical for me to simply present [his] view of himself
and the world as true and accurate. I felt compelled to consti-
tute an image of him and his actions consistent with my own
ethical principles.

As the months passed … I attempted to share my concerns
[with him], but he successfully evaded my efforts.

Before commenting on Sharon's experience, Dana's dilemma is worth
sharing. It is grounded in the context of a researcher who has articulated an
explicit purpose to her respondents only to encounter, as a result of data collection–analysis–interpretation, difficulty in honoring that purpose fully.
Hers is a study of "six young white women teachers in an urban setting trying to come to terms with their own ambiguous position with regard to students, parents, and administrators."

A more problematic area of this experience for me was
grappling with ethical dilemmas surrounding qualitative
research. Specifically, I was troubled by the conflicting social and professional prerogatives of my research. As I
worked with the teachers who participated in my study, I
felt a range of emotions. I respected their commitment and
ingenuity. I admired their skillful management and negoti-
ation of a variety of challenging situations. I appreciated
the untold hours they spent working with students, preparing special activities and lessons, etc. I was grateful for

their generosity in opening their classrooms and taking time to talk with me. In our conversations, I always tried to highlight their strengths and successes. When they faced difficulties, I noted the structural and cultural impediments that were outside their control.

However, when I began to analyze my complete data set and write the dissertation, I was confronted by what seemed to me an ugly truth: The teachers were sometimes complicit in their own difficulties. Unwittingly, they made their own circumstances worse in quite a few situations. I felt that in order to fulfill my stated purpose of documenting their experience, I needed to include this component of the story. However, to do so—in effect, to call attention to false consciousness or simple naivete—would be a violation of the spirit of our time together. *I had presented myself, accurately, as a young woman champion of young women teachers, someone eager to spell out their particular circumstances in an empathetic and supportive way. How could one of my findings be that these teachers exacerbated their own problems?* [italics added]

Like Sharon, Dana stated her purposes and expectations up front, that is, each presented her best sense and understanding of her role with her respondents at the beginning of the research. Sharon discussed "nonintervention" as one of her ethical guidelines; as highlighted in the italicized portion of Dana's letter, Dana was to be "a champion" of her respondents' experiences. These examples suggest that our initial self-presentation can end up leaving us with little "wiggle room" as our research unfolds. What we <u>don't</u> know about a lot of things emerges as we encounter new experience; what we <u>do</u> know and understand then changes. An ethical dilemma can emerge when the limitations of our now past states of knowing "emerge."

Both Sharon and Dana have made explicit one of the qualities of the qualitative; the great trouble and great gift of qualitative research is how very much we learn—not solely about the context—in the undertaking of it. Experienced qualitative researchers, like Sharon and Dana have become, are not immune from such occurrences. Yet, as Dana writes in the closing of her letter, "I don't have clear answers for these questions, but they are certainly issues that I will consider explicitly in preparing to do future research."

QUESTIONS

8. Have you had a course in or concrete experience with ethics? Is a course available at your university? If not, how do you intend to acquire, learn about, debate, and finally determine your ethical stance as a qualitative researcher?

9. How clearly can you articulate your philosophical–ideological, moral and ethical stances? How idealistic are you? How realistic?

10. Have you ever had to defend your stances in action? If yes, what conclusions did you draw? What strengths emerged in your self-understanding? If no, would you be willing to attempt to articulate them and invite challenge in order to help you sort through thinking and doing? Do you have "critical friends" or supportive professors to work with?

11. If you hold feminist or critical perspectives, for example, how aware are you of the expectations and subsequent actions such perspectives will ask of you?

12. If you wish "only" to describe, are you off the "ethical hook"?

13. Regardless of your answers to questions eleven and twelve, how able are you to confront injustice when you come upon it? How willing are you to describe "warts and all"? Is qualitative research for you?

14. Are you beginning to sense that knowing your ethical stance is a requisite, but not the only step in preparing for contexts rife with discrepancy?

15. Have you taken the Myers–Briggs or a thinking styles inventory? Are you a judger or a perceiver? A thinker or a feeler? Is your thinking style concrete sequential or abstract random? Would a self-awareness inventory be help-

ful as you contemplate who you are in relationship to your work with others? Why or why not?

Sharon's chapter includes several mentions of attempts to check draft analyses and interpretations with her research participant. Dana found this aspect of her work a focal point for additional concern.

> A second dilemma arose as I completed a draft. Although I had not promised the teachers the chance to review my work, I felt that I should share it with them. I mailed each teacher a copy of the draft, invited her to respond to it, and then wrote an epilogue based on the feedback. A few teachers had factual corrections to make. Some offered additional examples or extensions on ideas I had included. Most were very positive about the experience of reading the dissertation. One said that she felt validated by my work, and another said that it was helpful to read. Still another teacher said that it was "exactly right" and that she had recognized herself in other teachers' stories.
>
> However, two teachers were clearly surprised and upset by portions of my rendering. One said that the chapter about her was hard to read because is seemed cynical and one-sided. Another teacher felt that important context was missing from quotations attributed to her. She felt that she had been depicted as a racist, and she said of her alias, "That can't be me."
>
> Few reactions are more disturbing to a qualitative researcher than these. I set out to report on young women teachers with a commitment to accuracy and fairness. I actively solicited feedback from the teachers at multiple points during the process of collecting data. Even so, and perhaps inevitably, their reception of my analysis was mixed.
>
> Several teachers took the opportunity to provide additional information that might enhance or alter my understanding. I

began eagerly writing down anything they could tell me with the intent to revise. The more I thought about this process, however, the more troubled I was by it. Is retrospective information amplifying or contaminating? ... In the situation of alleged racism, I wanted to make explicit the possible effects of idealistic young teachers adopting a stance of color-blindness. The teacher wanted to make sure that she was not depicted as a bigot. I focused on the notion of a case study, a specific instance that might be part of a larger pattern. The teacher, even though she was anonymous, was attuned to the notion of *her* life story. After all, a case study is a case, but it is also about someone. In attempting to do right by the teachers, how do I weigh palatability against rigor? Now *there's* a qualitative issue.

Edwina also struggles with reaction to her work.

An ethical issue that I still face if I want to publish is that several of my colleagues displayed ignorance of—and at times a haughty disdain for—theories and strategies for improving the teaching of writing. Even though they would not be identified, they would recognize themselves; although they may not recognize their own statements as negative or counterproductive, my interpretations may offend. And yet, how do we ever change things in the teaching profession? Must change be confrontational? Where is effective teaching in this conundrum?

The fear of offending, whether respondents or colleagues, remains an issue many qualitative researchers face. Suffering the imagined consequences of our actions can lead to inaction; ignoring the potential consequences of our inaction can lead to pain.

SUMMARY

Anticipating dilemmas does become easier with experience, but experience does not preclude them from possibility. Clarifying your ethical–methodological–ideological stances ahead of time is one way to gain "experience" with what you might encounter. Additionally, correspondents for both editions of this volume have mentioned the value of pilot studies and early writings as means of gaining valuable competence and confidence prior to undertaking the dissertation research itself.

I chose to close this chapter with the contributions on ethics because I believe our inner resources—our beliefs, philosophies, senses of care and responsibility—guide and support our research as well as any set of specific skills. Part of the rigor, part of the responsibility is to know one's self. Leslie Bloom's (1999) contribution to the *International Qualitative Studies in Education Journal* is one example of the introspection—and retrospection—a seasoned qualitative researcher is willing to bring to her work.

7

UNDERSTANDING BY WRITING

Voice, "Emotional Journey," Journals

Take some risks in your writing. I didn't feel comfortable
with a completely alternative format for my dissertation; at
the same time, my use of metaphors, poetic transcription,
and an impressionist tale was exciting and invigorating to
me. I really enjoyed searching for quotes from my interviewees that could be used in part as headings or descriptions of themes. Each of these approaches took my writing
in some new directions and made me feel that my work was
more creative and unique than I had imagined it could be.
I'd like in the future to experiment further, but at the time I
was writing, I found these modes of expression to be challenging but not so threatening as to make me feel that I had
gone totally beyond my comfort zone. (Katie)

One of the major changes in this edition is the increased attention the correspondents put on the subject of writing. It is they who have convinced me
that the linkages voiced in the first edition (i.e., learning–thinking–writing)
are being strongly forged in programs supportive of qualitative research.
Correspondents in the first edition responded to a probe about "keeping a
journal." Although I did not ask the same questions for this edition, several
correspondents did mention their journals. But it is my sense of our work together that although a journal provides an opportunity for writing, it is only
one location or focus for a discussion about writing. By now you have noticed many thoughts about writing throughout this book. In order to honor
its presence most directly, I will begin this chapter with a lengthy excerpt
from one of Katie's letters and then conclude with the topic of journals. I
would like to add, however, that this change in emphasis does <u>not</u> signify a

change in my belief about the value of a journal; on the contrary, I remain convinced—given the excerpts Mary K. and Helen share later in this chapter—that journals can play a significant role in the thinking–reflecting–analysis–interpretation–understanding process.

VOICE

Without a prompt, Katie wrote mostly about writing. Her thoughts offer a clear and comprehensive overview to the topic. That she relates her learning about writing while doing it suggests the integral connection of doctoral course work to the final "product." Writing as connected to the topic of "voice" is another theme Katie describes in detail.

> In some ways, the fact that I worked from four case study reports developed prior to the official start of my dissertation study meant that I had written things before I really started writing. The notion that "thinking is writing" and "writing is thinking" and thus, that writing/thinking begins before "official" writing begins is something I have thought about and tried to practice since reading Henry Wolcott (1990) in one of my research methods classes. The writing of my dissertation began with those four case studies and continued with short pieces I had written as part of our larger research project, as well as a reflection on research paradigms that I wrote about for one of our doctoral core courses, and a chapter that I began in one course and finished in another, in which we wrote and rewrote a piece throughout the course. So on the day that I "officially" began to write, I found that I had already written a lot. That was a good feeling! I defended my dissertation about 4 months after its official beginning, but as I look back, I can see that I started writing about 3 years prior to my defense....
>
> *So once I knew that I was meant to be a qualitative researcher ...*

I had to learn some new things.... I had to learn how to write in the first person (a practice banned by my teachers since the sixth grade), and, closely related to this, how to make my voice part of my writing. Moreover, I had to feel that I *had* a voice. The latter was a journey related to my dissertation work, but also borne before it, albeit through some painful and wonderful processes like divorce, remarriage, and the raising of children. I was amazed at the power of writing in the first person. I remember sharing one draft of my chapter on caring during a class.... The week prior to the class, my group of "critical friends" had suggested they couldn't hear enough of me. I came back the following week, my writing smattered with the word "I," and (I thought), full of my own voice. I attached a sheet to my new draft—"Where's Katie?" it said, in big letters (something I borrowed from the books titled "Where's Waldo?"). To my surprise, they still claimed not to hear me, so I kept adding more.

There were more evolutions in my writing ...

such as the week we were talking about alternative ways to present qualitative studies and Corinne [our professor] related her experiences with creating poems out of transcripts of interviews—hence, "poetic transcription." I rejected the idea at first. I wasn't sure I could do it—it seemed too contrived. But as I drove home from class that night, I heard the voices of some students I'd interviewed and I suddenly knew that their voices made a poem.... For me, it was a highlight of my writing experience. It was the most "different" thing that I did.... I was amazed to find how easily the voices of the students came together to make a poem. I did very little other than alter some tenses and pronouns, and I was thrilled to find two students in two schools describing their school in nearly the same words. I put one of their lines at the beginning of the poem and one at the end. In between, I created stanzas out of main ideas (e.g., thoughts about teachers, thoughts about receiving help from teachers, thoughts about hard things at school and things that could be changed). To me, the poem gave concrete testimony to the spirit of caring that I'd observed and felt in each of their schools and saw as central to the fact that these schools were identified as exemplars with respect to meeting the needs of all students. The poem glued together my impressions, the data, and my themes [see Glesne, 1999, pp. 186–187]. I remember talking later with someone about a fear I had, that maybe I saw too many connections among things. The wise person countered that finding connections is what research and life should be about. For me, the poem gave substance to connections I'd been thinking and writing about—more testimony to Wolcott's idea that writing is thinking and to Corrine's contention that creative approaches to writing may serve to deepen the thinking process.

I stretched my writing capacities again by trying my hand at writing an "impressionist tale" (Van Maanan, 1988) at the outset of the chapter that included the poem. The tale was an attempt to capture the essence of one school I had been visiting by relating images, smells, sounds, and impressions in a writing style that approximated a stream of consciousness. In addition to thinking of the tale as a way to provide a context for the chapter, I also thought of it as a way to introduce themes that I'd return to later using a more academic style of writing. I really enjoyed putting this piece together; the writing gave me the same kind of satisfaction I used to derive from writing short stories and "books."

Another important learning for me in the writing process was the way in which I began to learn how to weave the literature into my writing without obscuring my voice. At first, simply figuring out what literature to read and to include in my dissertation challenged me. There's a lot out there—I could easily have read forever. Corrine had forewarned us about this. She said our reviews of the literature would be based on the processes of induction, intuition, and evolution. I loved these words, but I wasn't sure how it could all fit. My habit has generally been to do too much anyway. But I learned how to do this, I think. I read lots of the literature around my major themes, but I by no means read all of it. I did three independent, small group studies as part of my doctoral program in which I (and sometimes a partner or two) developed reading lists related to my themes, read, and wrote about what I had read, often in the form of "one-pagers." When it came time to write my dissertation literature review, I thus felt reasonably knowledgeable about a number of things (I learned that one must feet comfortable in being a generalist, at least much of the time, in the qualitative process). I was still concerned, however, about how to articulate my process of reviewing the literature and my decisions about what to include, until that "where's Katie" thing hit me again. I realized that even though I was writing a literature review and thus, a somewhat traditional part of my dissertation, I could still drag out my voice long enough to talk about my reading process and decisions. In fact, I think my review of the literature was much better for this, as I was able shape it in accordance with the things I was thinking about when I read them. As it turned out, the review summarizes both the content of what I read and thought to be most important, as well as the thinking processes I engaged in as I learned.

Katie mentions themes other correspondents have also thought about, including voice and ownership, writing in first person, the literature review, and so forth. Perhaps this chapter is the place for them. Jean writes:

A friend (who is now a faculty member at another university) and I took my first and her only qualitative research methods course together. She is an incredible statistician. If I want to do anything with statistics, I'll turn to her. She understands qualitative research and why it is done. She chooses not to do it because she does not feel she writes well enough. If a student comes to her with a problem that involves qualitative research, she will guide the student to someone who conducts qualitative research and writes well. She will do this not because she isn't capable but because this is not where her passion or expertise lies. She and I have had many discussions surrounding this issue and have decided that a qualitative researcher must be a writer. She doesn't feel that writing is as important in quantitative studies.... A well-written statistical paper is a gift and great, but the use or abuse of the statistical data is what matters. I know that she and I respect each other as teachers, researchers, and scholars. We have both come away from the class and our discussions with a healthy respect for the amount of work involved in conducting any research.

Kathy also reflected on voice:

Everyone on my committee has encouraged writing in the first person from the beginning, but I interpreted their expectations to include expository rather than narrative writing. I got hung up with my perceptions of the expectations of the committee members that would be reading the study. At one point, I wanted to be told what to include and how to write it and was willing to give up my own voice, a voice expressed through style and content and the freedom to try it out my way. It was not until I felt that I was deadlocked and totally unsure of the expectations of others and decided to finish without any other advice or criticism and then let people react, that I discovered my own voice, a voice that was reflected in a more confident writing style, my writing style. Prior drafts had been written with individual faculty members as the intended audience and were influenced by other studies considered as possible models.

Claiming ownership of our work can conflict with learning about how to do our work and learning what others expect. I had an undergraduate student walk into my office at the end of last semester and tell me that I, and a colleague in the English department, were the only two professors for whom he "couldn't write. I don't know what you want." He did not care for my response. I told him I wanted to him to write clearly and well; I wanted him to build an argument and defend it. "Make you points, connect them, convince me," I replied. "Don't write for me," I said, "write to me—from you."

EMOTIONAL JOURNEY

There is something contradictory about coming back to school as an adult, after confidence and "success" have already been a part of our lives, and "beginning" again. The investment we make to learn again at a different level requires new and different skills; it can lead us to doubt our past and question our future. Many correspondents describe the volatile emotional journey writing a qualitative dissertation is. Direct statements about how this experience feels are made throughout the chapters of this book. Dana deals directly with one aspect of this "trip."

> I suspect that the stance of many dissertation writers is fear. We fear being found wanting on account of insufficient rigor in our background research, methodology, fieldwork, or analysis.... But fear is not the muse of clear and confident writing.

As we moved toward the close of the second edition in the summer of 2000, one correspondent confided the following, suggesting Dana might be right.

> I'm a little pleased that your project may be taking longer than you planned, since this dissertation I am trying to write is the biggest weight around my neck I have ever faced ... and I'm 41! I had no idea this last step would be so painful and so lonely.

For this edition, several correspondents addressed the challenges of writing a qualitative dissertation. The first letter from the correspondent just excerpted hinted at explicit emotional connections from the very beginning.

I am writing in response to your request for participation in the revision of your book. I know that I am writing to you well past your deadline.... Every week I thought I could muster the courage to write, and well, the weeks would pass.... I needed to write you when I could do so emotionally, and today is that day....

I could probably go on and on ... but I'll get to the heart of my experience writing my dissertation. Or shall I say, not writing my dissertation.

After passing the comprehensive exams I took one more class, initiated some relationships with possible participants for my dissertation, and then froze. I gladly stopped the 4-hour round trips to campus a couple times a week, and re-engaged my professional consulting life and quickly embraced routine day-to-day family activities. I had, and still have, a "full life" that I very much enjoy.

The months passed. And the guilt began. And then my advisor, my lone program contact at this distant university died suddenly. My friend, my colleague, and my umbilical cord to graduate student life and process was gone. I cried. I felt sorry for myself. I grieved with other peers at the funeral. It took me 4 months before I could face the task of reconfiguring my committee.

My home department has been supportive....

I tend to always look for the very best in every life experience.... But being so removed from campus, without a peer group, and unseasoned as a researcher, I feel pretty lonely. My self-confidence, never a problem, has weighed in on my assessment of, "can I do this?" ...

I find myself wanting to keep reading and reading and reading. Or, I love collecting data, spending time with my participants. Our rapport and time together is terrific.... But writing—oh how I have been procrastinating. I'm afraid to begin. Afraid to be wrong. I feel I should know so much more than what dribbles out onto the page.

At this writing my advisor and I have set a deadline for submission of the proposal to her and a follow-up date for presentation to my committee. I appreciate the concrete timeline and am anxious to proceed. Her telephone counsel has been great, but overall, by virtue of my life choices and this family I love, I do feel pretty alone. I would like more advice on what to do by when, and what to expect, and what I need to "know." I know that not knowing is part of what I love ... but I am struggling and I am, frankly, afraid. *If you knew me well, you would no doubt be stunned by this admission.* [italics added]

This correspondent is not alone; writing any kind of dissertation requires focus and commitment. Writing a qualitative dissertation genuinely feels more directly "from" or "of" us than does reporting the results of data input and statistical analysis.

Katie wrote earlier about finding voice as a researcher; finding voice as an advocate, as one who has learned something and is not "just telling stories" is another source of anxiety and is a theme across several letters for this edition. Jim writes:

I have no doubt that my [being in a parallel administrative position] at the time provided a common ground.... My dissertation speaks to issues I felt strongly about and that have very real application....

The problem is ... this stuff is hard work; because it has a fluid quality to it, it catches vast amounts of information. The analysis–synthesis process that must follow is just as difficult as the process that produced the design in the first place.

Diana recalls that "issues of voice and representation strike me as the most important and challenging aspects of my dissertation work.... My greatest struggle with the dissertation process revolved around issues of where to place myself within the research." Barbara writes that "the research must be meaningful to me in emotional ways, as well as in scientific, scholarly, and intellectual ways." Chris also writes of connection:

> My methodology evolved from being mainly an observer to being mainly a participant and coming to terms with the tensions between living my life (and making sense of things that have happened to me) and being a researcher (and thus making sense of what happens to others), particularly how each influences the other. My methodology ended up being highly reflective, defined in part by my making sense of my participation and the literature, both research and fiction, I was reading at the time.

Mary K. shared several e-mails with me beginning with her first response to my inquiry in the fall of 1998. I begin with her e-mail of November 7, 1998. I then interrupt that letter by inserting some of her background journal entries in order to support a better understanding of the November letter. I conclude with a lengthy excerpt from that letter.

> NOW, I will preface this and my future conversations to you with the following, borrowing book title and song lyric from whoever said it, (I'm more profound in my academic writing, trust me) "This much is true …"

1. You have editor's privilege (and spell check-smile) = YOU
2. You asked for willing participants (with opinions) = ME
   SO, with that said …

> Letter Interrupted

> (The following words are from my journal called, "The 'D' Process: Getting Started" which was started 10/23/95 (my emotions of the process; I put them on these pages so that my mind remains clear and focused.)

I'm reading *Emotions and Fieldwork* by Sherryl Kleinman and Martha A. Copp (1993). It's part of the process of preparing for the 2nd half of this journey. I'm pumped and ready to go. On page 57, the authors cite Elbow (1981) regarding the need to do "free writing" when the process begins, before the first phone call, the first visit. That is where I'll begin.

I need to call Lynne Hamer and talk to her about my idea. She had repeatedly said, during one of my qualitative research classes she taught, that I had a great idea for my study. I can finally understand what she was talking about....

11/6/95 I am not the one. I am not the spokesperson, cheerleader, or otherwise ambassador of good words regarding my experience as a graduate student.... I don't know when it started, but I know that there have been several reasons. Where do I begin to categorize these wicked thoughts, the destruction? *Politics and Ethics in Fieldwork* made some interesting points. I'm thinking at this point I don't even want to finish school. I must quickly eradicate this thought so I can get on with this madness.

11/14/95, 11:56 p.m. Swirling thoughts ... so much to do in so little time. Every Tuesday, I feel a slightly elevated sense of anxiety before and after Angie and I review for our major exams. I know that a month from today, I will be finished teaching these 5 classes ... as well as completed my involvement....

9/8/96, 6:23 a.m. Numbers or words? The dilemma begins. Quantitative or qualitative? Now I'm starting over. Back to the drawing board, but I have some terrific research behind me. I think much of what I've read and used has either helped to synthesize my topic to a workable size or it was just something good to know.

Letter of November 7, 1998, rejoined

So, with that said …

**CONSTIPATION … DIARRHEA … BOWEL
PROBLEMS … (statement of problem)

okay,

I'll bump it up a notch.

Literary C …

Literary D …

Literary BP …

Now, I'll frame my study.

Public LC

Public LD

Public LBP

DOCTORAL DISSERTATION PROCESS …

In a phrase and personal: "Preparing and releasing MY dissertation proposal to someone to read for the very first
time."

OK, that may be a little dramatic, but that's what my being
and my body has experienced since April 1995, when I
took the final course of my doctoral program that was SUP-
POSED to have, as the culminating project, a draft of my
dissertation proposal.… NOT!!!! [today is 11/7/98].… I
don't even have a grade in the course yet. I have a "PR,"
which means I'm still "in the process" of completing the

work. Have I been goofing off or just putting it off? NO!!! Have I thought about it almost every day since that class was over? YES!!! Have I felt wonderful about myself as a person, as a scholar, as an aspiring academician who will lead other students successfully through this "academic hazing process?" NO, NO, NO!!! I felt and still feel like an impostor.

So, when I recently heard the following words—"So, you just have to get that PhD, are you STILL working on that?"—I ALMOST exploded!!! But that, my dear Judy, is what you call a LAXATIVE, a LITERARY LAXATIVE … (and just for that, the count for the bound "Limited Edition" copies of my dissertation just increased by one!)

Judy, this is my prologue to our conversation; you wouldn't believe the words that are in my mind, in my fingers, in the cells of my being, in the follicles of my scalp, in every living particle of my body. Some of the words have escaped on the pages of the numerous (8–11) journals that I've kept during this state…. ALSO, I must admit, that on July 9 (1998) to be exact, I believe that my God saw that my case of PLC had reached epic, almost fatal, proportions. So do you know what my God did? You won't believe this. My God sent me AN ANGEL, my own Public Literary ANGEL. I didn't know it then, but I had met the person who would provide the softener to the academic, verbal, mental obstruction that plagued me for so long…. Because on July 10, 1998, I basically hit the delete button [a step courageously taken by my dear friend Jon a year earlier] and I started my dissertation almost from scratch … square one … the beginning … the inception…. On October 23, 1998, I finally released the first draft of my "dissertation proposal in progress" to one of my committee members to review…. It was a relief, but also one of those moments of vulnerability (all a part of the process).

Although Mary K. gave me editorial privilege, I edited only lightly, removing a few redundancies. As her first reader, I was struck by the enormity of Mary K.'s emotional, mental, physical, and spiritual experience. I also know Mary K.'s experience is <u>not</u> an anomaly, as much as I know that there are others who seem to float right through. Most of us experience both highs and lows. I am blessed by the candor of the correspondents' reflections, because they focus the image of "the researcher as the human instrument" more sharply than either a list of rules or set of skills necessary to accomplish the research well. They are telling it like it is.

Fear and vulnerability exist concomitantly with other emotions. As one correspondent wrote:

> Purposes and expectations aside, my experience was enlightening and frustrating—often simultaneously. On the one hand, I discovered that many ... had little, sometimes no, knowledge of teaching methods or their underlying theories ...; however, I also learned that sometimes methods are not the deciding factors for a successful student experience.

In part of the preface to Mary K.'s e-mail, she writes:

> The passion that sparked my desire to do research on this topic (retention of and support mechanisms for graduate students of color) remains fierce. The experience of living through the antithesis of what I hope my research will reveal about one such mechanism allows me to share this and other experiences with the authority gained as an African American woman with tremendous battle scares and emotional wounds that may never heal. This authority inspires me to do all within my abilities to prevent this experience from being unnecessarily replicated by another student of color in pursuit of his or her academic goal.

Mary K.'s passion and position reinforce the autobiographical nature of the work that several of the contributors to this volume have explicitly undertaken. You, who are choosing this work, will find its connections both personal and emotionally charged. But you must also know that <u>no one</u>

has written me to say "don't do it" or "it's not worth it," in spite of my invitation in the first edition to do so. I think that's because there appears to be so much satisfaction accomplishing one's goals in this way. Diana remembers:

> That I was "allowed" to write this personally in my dissertation reflects, I think, the support of my committee and especially my chairperson. More importantly, however, it provides a record—my record—of what it is like to write about my own life in the context of other similar lives. From the distance of a few years, I firmly believe this to be its greatest value. Writing a dissertation is (at least in part) an academic experience in learning to do research; in my case, it was much more than that—it was an experience in learning important lessons about myself.

And on a lighter note, another correspondent recalls:

> Among my fondest memories were my two formal defenses, the proposal–qualitative defense and the dissertation defense. I made both of these occasions "postfeminist." I served food and drink at each meeting, and actually had a sign in front of the food saying "Postfeminist Methodology."

JOURNAL

As clearly indicated by the samples from Mary K.'s journal, a journal can be a valuable tool for reflection and understanding. Mary K. writes: "I am keeping my journal with fieldnotes to process my concerns about this split perspective [qualitative–quantitative] that I work to bring to a singular existence in the form of my dissertation." Some people keep diaries and journals as a matter of personal choice. Other people are writers, or perhaps historians or note-takers who wish to remember particular events. During the course of thesis research, many of the correspondents found, as I did, that keeping a journal in some form was worth doing. It became a resource of our own creation and experience; it held our hearts. You will notice as you read that there appear to be a variety of definitions of "journal"; the question posed earlier, "What's in a name?" is an issue here. Although the following excerpts will probably not help you formulate the "definitive" journal, they will offer a number of possibilities from which you might choose.

Many correspondents responded to this topic in their letters, as I had specifically asked in my original letter, "Do or did you keep a journal?" Ann replies in the affirmative.

> Yes, I am keeping a journal. My advisor wasn't particularly impressed by my wanting to keep a journal or notes on the research process. More work. After an interview, I have at times found it tedious to write up a description of the person interviewed and the experience of what I am finding, but I have mostly enjoyed examining my navel and best of all, found it valuable to look at my notes later as I proceed with analysis. I was delighted to find that reading the description in my journal of a woman I had interviewed 2 months ago really brought her to life again for me as well as the experience of interviewing her.

Later, she adds:

> At first, for perhaps 1 month, I wrote everything up in a lined book as if I was writing a research diary. I also had separate pages taken from a separate folder in which I kept the accounts of each interview. Then I happened to reread Bogdan and Biklen (1982) and was reminded of the techniques they suggest for keeping research notes in their "data analysis" chapter. Based on their suggestions, I now have:

1) A journal in which I write up accounts of initial contact and interviews. Beyond description, I try to include an account of what I found out in that interview; for instance, did I find anything striking? Was there an image that stood out? Did something a person said remind me of another interview? I make a note if there is anything I want to ask the

next interviewee or if there are other ideas I should try out. I write this up directly after an interview.

2) I also have a research journal (like a diary). I write this at the end of each day. Here I try to comment or reflect on what I am learning methodwise, what I am learning substancewise, and perhaps see if I can make connections with theory. I might also have a bright idea about the way to describe something that is going on in the research.

Robert is enthusiastic about his decision to keep a journal:

> I kept a journal and urge others to do so. It provides a forum from which hypotheses emerge. By reviewing accumulated data (and clutter!) one sees themes emerging. It also provides the putty to fill in holes or a basis for tossing out ideas—not enough or contradictory information to support hypotheses. In short, it was a sounding board. I reviewed mine recently and, after 2 years, I can still see how my thoughts proceeded from inklings to full-blown conclusions.

My own effort at keeping a journal falls somewhere between Ann's and Robert's. I did "flesh out" my interview interactions immediately after each interview. I wanted to be sure I captured our interaction in detail. I added these thoughts about "fact" and "perception" directly into my field notes. Then, on the long drive home or in the solitude of the inviting guest room provided by a wonderful, intelligent, and caring couple I had only just met, I would talk into my tape recorder about everything that was going on in my head. Method combined with feelings combined with hunches combined with doubts combined with ideas. Back on campus, I would transcribe the tapes. Then I went through the ramblings and sorted them into their own categories—feelings, themes, areas to probe, frustrations, and so forth emerged from the "dump." I consider fleshing out the interview notes as part of my "official" responsibility as a researcher. After I had taken the time account for our interaction as accurately as I could, I then felt "free" to let out all my reactions to that experience and let my mind wander in the possibilities. Hence, although I can see the value in keeping two journals, I really only kept one—my field notes and my tape-recorded talk and ramblings; this strategy seems natural to me.

Paula also thinks it's a good idea to keep a journal:

> Yes, I kept a journal. It is like a diary with feelings and frustrations included in the entries. There is probably a lot of insight in my journal entries. I believe that a journal is a "must" for qualitative research studies. The journal entries acted as a catharsis, releasing my tension, renewing my spirits, and bringing to consciousness my thoughts, emotions, and fears. I wrote in it during the data collection and analysis phases of my study. I went back to it during analysis to read various entries, which enabled me to draw some conclusions.

Kathryn relates that her journal was particularly useful when she began focusing on a thesis topic:

> To answer your question about the journal, I think I should summarize how I came to identify my research topic. I summarized each quarter of my clinical work in a formal paper. I reconstructed this summary from the notes I kept during clinical experiences. (My program had a strong clinical orientation; I used the summaries of 20 quarter hours of clinical work to focus on my area of clinical and research interest.) So, while I really did not think of it as keeping a journal, my notes served that purpose. I also kept notes during the analysis phase of my research in order to clarify <u>why</u> [emphasis added] I was thinking something so I could go back later and reconstruct. What was interesting about this is sometimes I labored over these decisions and when I came back to them later, I was surprised how clear it was to me. I think keeping notes in itself forced the thought processes.

Not all correspondents had great luck with or kept journals; a few kept other kinds of supporting records. Pat writes:

> I tried to keep a journal, but it was poorly done. Because I could relive the episode on tape, I did little journaling. Re-

flection was, more appropriately, my method of focusing my research perspective. I found that although I had spent much time in my own classroom, only when I was able to "step around the desk" and be a part of the play did I come to know the children as human beings. My reflection forced my thinking and sent me to additional readings as I searched for those who looked at young children as part of the culture.

Patricia did not keep a journal of her experiences. Kristin's effort sounds similar to my own: "I didn't keep a journal but did write 'notes on notes' after I transcribed interviews and wrote field notes. In these notes I talked about categories emerging in the data, comparisons with the other sites, and my emotions about the fieldwork." Nancy's experience offers another option.

I did not keep a personal journal of the dissertation experience. I kept careful records while conducting my mini-case study—of my interviews, observations, etc.—labeling them with date, place, actors, and any pertinent information (such as the explosion of the Challenger shuttle, which occurred during the lunch hour and just before I interviewed someone who had seen the TV report).

Gretchen responds differently by writing, "I did not keep a journal, and of course now I wish I had." In the following excerpt, Jean uses almost the exact same language; I remain curious as to why both of these correspondents might do things differently today.

I did not keep a journal of my process, although I wish now that I had. I kept a teaching journal and a very private journal (which I have since destroyed) at the time I was working on the dissertation, but I did not have time for a journal of my process. (I was ill during part of the time I was working on my dissertation and had to face major surgery. I kept a private journal concerning that process which I used to "vent my spleen." My husband was very supportive throughout everything and knew I kept that journal. He knows that it was destroyed after it had served its purpose.)

I have kept the teaching journal and may use that sometime in the future in some form of research.

Still another correspondent remembers the research experience:

No, I did not keep a journal, but I did write all of these things into the text of my thesis, which is a running narrative of why decisions were made (logic, necessity, bureaucratic constraints) and of the tradeoffs I made. For example, the choice of one participant for my study was very risky, for that person had an intense crush on me and revealed it to me. I am fairly comfortable with such things, having experienced them myself, but that was one of the potential "problems" I discussed with my advisor. It could have exploded in my face, and my degree with it. It could have been hard to be "objective" (not quite the right word, I think, but you know what I mean). It could also have been an asset because of the nature of the openness between us, and, in fact, that was what occurred. My advisor left the decision entirely up to me, and I did exactly what I wanted to.

QUESTIONS

1. Whose decision is it to keep a journal? Yours? Your advisor's?
2. What are the advantages of keeping a journal? The disadvantages?
3. Is "examining one's navel" of particular benefit to qualitative researchers? If so, must the reflections be written down? Are peer debriefing or taping thoughts while driving viable alternatives?
4. "Bringing to consciousness" is one aspect of the doing–thinking–writing–discovering–understanding pro-

cess that is qualitative research. Does writing force or encourage reflection—or does reflection enable writing?

5. Can you separate product from process? Is it important to—or not to? Why or why not?
6. Do you like to write?

SUMMARY

An essential theme of this book is that writing is an integral part of what qualitative research is all about. The title of this volume has never seemed so clearly accurate on a variety of levels. For some, keeping track of personal feelings and professional experience provides ongoing support for and confirmation of the process; however, as Maria suggests, doing so may not be for everyone.

> In regard to your question about keeping a journal, my advisor encouraged all of us to do so. Some members of the dissertation study group did. I must confess, I never did, and even though I came to regret it, I still cannot bring myself to keep journals on other issues I am researching.

In the few pages that follow, the journal of correspondent Helen Rolfe may provide some clues as to why Maria might "regret" not keeping one. Although labeled "Notes on Methodology" and included as Appendix F in her dissertation, I believe Helen's writing offers a strong example of the multifaceted reflections a human being experiences when he or she is the research instrument within the particular context of a study. Helen has pulled examples from her field notes to highlight a variety of questions, learnings, and growing understandings of methodological issues and personal concerns. Helen's contribution points to the importance of note-taking and reflection during the process of qualitative research for the doctoral dissertation.

APPENDIX F

NOTES ON METHODOLOGY

As the study progressed, I had many thoughts about what was happening as I met and interviewed people in the two schools. These notes represent some themes that ran through the field notes taped after each data-collection occurrence.

Emergent design. Into the study, it became apparent what "emergent design" meant. As much as I had anticipated in the proposal, changes were inevitable once the data collection began. The research proposal, seemingly airtight and sensible when it passed the scrutiny of the committee, has been modified, trimmed, and shaped in the actual doing of this study. You cannot anticipate the events that will cause you to have to change what you have outlined to do.... I have not been able to be in the schools every 2 weeks. My visits have been much more like monthly (field notes, 4/29/88).

Unwilling participants. One teacher was very reluctant to be taped. I persuaded her to talk with me with the tape running, with the understanding that if she was not happy, she could opt out of the study. By the end of the interview she seemed very relaxed and amenable to my coming for an observation of a lesson, a sign to me that the interview had gone well. Other cases did not end so well. It was disappointing not to have the central office coordinator participate in the study. In my haste to set up a meeting with her, I had my secretary call and make the appointment. There was a misunderstanding about my purpose for the meeting with her, and it contributed to her refusal to participate, I think.

Interview technique. Early in the study I was overcome with how hard it was to restrain myself in interviews. I had to bite my tongue several times, and I was unsuccessful other times, trying to keep from putting words in his mouth, to draw conclusions for him. It's real important that these folks have the opportunity to draw their own conclusions about what they're telling me (field notes, 2/1/88).

Sometimes the tape recorder intruded on interviews. At one point I had a strong desire to be less obtrusive with it. It would be nice to have a tape recorder that looked like an orchid, or a corsage. You just put it on, and say, "Speak into the flower bud, please" (field notes, 2/29/88).

Silence is an effective technique, I found. In one interview there were several times when the person cut an answer off and then was silent. I remained silent, too. Then she added something more. I think it's important to let someone talk, even if that person is somewhat uncomfortable with the idea of talking (field notes, 3/17/88).

First interviews. At the beginning of the study in each site there was an initial awkwardness in the first interviews. I didn't have a sense of what was going on in the school. It was as though I needed to have an event or happening, some entry point, so to speak, on which to focus questions. Once I had learned something about each school, it was easier to ask about current happenings as I eased into the interviews. That I felt a need to establish a shared understanding for the context with the persons whom I interviewed is a confirmation of the groundedness of qualitative research. The fact is that knowledge of how X was implemented could not be divorced from the context in which it occurred....

The importance of viewpoint. After interviewing her, it was impressed on me that what one learns about the subject at hand depends entirely on the person to whom one is talking. The view I was shown by her of what was going on was a very different picture from the one painted by another. It contradicted in almost every way the impression the other created.

Participant's reactions. With few exceptions there was very little feedback from any participants on the transcripts of interviews throughout the study. As we talked there was almost no probing of my intent.... At the end of the study, especially at one site, participants wanted to know what I would do with the results of the data collection.

Relationship between researcher and participants. One source of bias in qualitative research occurs when the researcher identifies with the participants in the study. I was not immune to personal involvement at one of the sites. By April, 1988, my field notes report this, in passing: "I really valued her input, because I believe in this site." I had to watch how I interacted with one or two persons, because of how easy it was to talk to them.

"She is pretty uninhibited and up front, an easy interview. So easy, you have to watch for what she doesn't say" (field notes, 5/4/88).

Rigors of the methodology. It was not always easy to know what was going on. One person described what she was doing, but as I reflected on it going home, it sounded like a home-grown curriculum with little attention to learner objectives. That's the way it sounds to me. It may not be that way. But how do you know? You listen to what a person says. You ask. You look. Then you trust your instincts (field notes, 5/6/88).

People talk to you and they either (a) communicate well, giving you one impression, or (b) communicate poorly, leaving another impression. Then you observe and see (c) what people were talking about, or (d) other things, not mentioned....

There was often a piercing sense of uncertainty about what I should be doing. That feeling came to the surface in one of the last interviews, when I found myself saying aloud things I had not to that point admitted to myself. Everything I have done is something new, and I have found that I am often very much afraid. If I move to a new phase, the first thing I have to get over is the feeling that I don't want to do this, because I am afraid (a) that I don't know what to do, and (b) that I won't do it right. I have found that once I get through that, then I get in and somehow things pull together (interview, 11/11/88).

Knowing when to end. After a year's investigation of the topic it was not hard to recognize signs pointing to the end of the study. I was suddenly overcome with the feeling that there wasn't any point in my talking with him anymore. I don't have lingering questions about his views or his interpretation of events for this fall. So I simply said, "I've just come by to ask you whether you think we need to talk again." He didn't, and I thanked him for helping me out (field notes, 12/19/88).

Analysis as an intuitive process. I suppose the process of analysis I used should be called intuitive; it was certainly not mechanical. Although throughout the study there were strong indications of themes within and across sites, the process remained a mystery, revealed only as it happened. There was no way for me to anticipate what would happen. My field notes said things like "Maybe the analysis will … Who knows?"

I constantly read and reread notes and interviews to steep myself in the information. Insights about what it meant came from somewhere, but I was never sure where. It was not difficult to support the ideas and thoughts I came up with, but they seemed to appear whole, in clusters, not piecemeal with lines attached to antecedents.

Personal feelings. I've gotten an absolutely wonderful start here. Coming home, my adrenaline was flowing. I was on a real high, because this interview today led me so

quickly into what they're doing that it gives me a rich background against which to lay other perceptions of the program (field notes, 1/2/88).

I was suddenly overwhelmed with the realization that there
are 6 weeks left. It was like a ton of bricks. That this study is
going to end is overwhelming to me at this point…. You're
never going to get to the end of the story, especially on
something as complicated as this study. I am wanting to tie
up all the loose ends, and it's impossible to do. I'm having
that fear of withdrawal I suppose any researcher has. I feel
guilty, naturally I suppose, about not having collected more
data … (field notes, 11/1/88).

I worried a lot about maintaining the confidentiality of participants. This question of maintaining confidentiality and
anonymity is a vexing one. My peer debriefer did a good
job of establishing a pseudonym right at the beginning. If I
were going to do this again, I would do the same thing: At
the initial point assign another name and use it throughout
the study (field notes, 11/1/88).

I hoped the issue of confidentiality would pass with time.
Will there ever come a time, say 4 years down the line,
when these data are old enough, far enough from the imme-
diacy of the situation so that I can go back and write a fuller
picture of the implementation in these schools? Maybe a
lot of that will come out in the analysis. Who knows? (field
notes, 11/28/88).

One reason I believe Helen's contribution to this book is important is because she has made explicit some of the seemingly "little" thoughts qualitative researchers have as they live and interact in the research setting. I
remember how everything I did, thought, or felt seemed to be of conse-
quence; I wasn't sure how to sort, what to leave in and what to leave out. The
contributions of Helen and the other correspondents, in their vulnerability
and openness, enable the neophyte researcher to have a sense of what it
"feels" like to be engaged in the context of a study. Perhaps even more im-

portantly, the range of experiences and interactions discussed throughout this book support the conception of multiple constructions of reality and the possibility of honing in on the nature and type of experiences that will bring more "quality" to qualitative research. Which thoughts and insights will enhance any one individual's efforts will be up to the individual as well as those in the profession interested in pushing further and knowing more. If, indeed, we learn by doing, then the value of keeping a journal may not be appreciated until the process is close to completion. In other words, understanding aspects of present practice will be fostered in future, if not simultaneous, reflection. That we do not always "know" or appreciate now does not mean we won't come to understand later.

8

UNDERSTANDING
BY DOING

Methodology, Analysis, and So Forth

> I agree with Bogdan and Biklen (1982) that most books on
> qualitative research don't write well on analysis. (Ann)

I think one of the reasons Ann comments on analysis is because the processes of qualitative research are multiple; they are linked and interactive,
to each other and to the human being who is the research instrument. Activities, such as reading, thinking, researching, writing, redoing and/or re-
thinking and writing, do not occur in a vacuum; lots of activity occurs
simultaneously. Unlike the systematic progression of selecting a particular
design and following the formulas for generating significance, the image of
progress in qualitative research is more like one of those crazy clocks, the
hour and minute hands of which revolve sometimes clockwise, sometimes
counterclockwise, sometimes together, and most often in opposition, so
that movement forward is not comfortingly, logically visible. We become
dizzy just watching it, and "dizzy" is sometimes exactly how individuals
doing qualitative research for their theses feel.

METHODOLOGY AND SELF

Because qualitative research requires personal rather than detached en-
gagement in context, it requires multiple, simultaneous actions and reactions from the human being who is the research instrument. As suggested in
the previous chapter, writing is one way to make visible what appears to be
going on. Talking into a tape recorder or with a friend or colleague is another means of "bringing to consciousness," which is partly analysis and
partly enabling of the process of analysis. But even something as

taken-for-granted as writing or talking has major consequences as decisions are made during the interaction of persons, method, and analysis. Personal style mingles with methodological implications—for instance, how is "ownership" different from bias or subjectivity? Is there a difference? Decisions about writing, such as voice and tense, get messed up with other decisions, such as where or when does the researcher's voice come in? How much of it is "appropriate?" Should it be there at all? Earlier excerpts from the correspondents have foreshadowed this issue. Harry Wolcott (1990) addressed questions like these in his book; others, including Colleen Larson (1992), Merry Merryfield (1992), John K. Smith (1992), Nancy Zeller (1990), Tom Barone (1992a, 1992b, 1993) and I (Meloy, 1992) have thought about these questions as well. It appears from a first glance at Kelly's letter that these questions do not pertain to her:

> My inquiry involves developing a collective case study of six women academics that have experience being first-generation college students from working class or poor backgrounds. My primary mode of inquiry involved conducting individual, semistructured feminist interviews. I developed an interview guide that helped move the interview conversation through a three-part series of open ended questions (Seidman, 1998). In brief I was interested in exploring the women's narratives that described their formative background experiences, their journeys into and through higher education, and their sense of self in relationship to these events and life choices. In the course of analysis, I considered their narratives from a perspective that took into consideration issues of class, gender, sexuality, and ethnicity. I should give you a brief sampling snapshot: three women are White, one woman is Jewish, and two women are Hispanic. One woman identified herself as lesbian. Two women considered their socioeconomic status growing up as one of "poverty." The remaining four described their families as working class. All have earned their doctorate and hold faculty positions in research universities. Data collection involved observation, document review, and in-depth individual interviews. I interviewed each woman three

times; each of the three interviews lasted approximately 2–3 hours. The interviews were audiotaped and transcribed verbatim. Transcripts were coded, chunked, and analyzed with the idea that themes would eventually emerge across their stories. Thank goodness; that's precisely what happened! My write-up and consequent interpretations were largely guided by these collective themes.

What you don't know is that Kelly chose to write me using the following organizational format: "I guess I will start with the more concrete aspects of this [work].... I will follow with some of the more subjective aspects." The connections to self, choice, and voice can be found in chapter 6.

Like Kelly, Linda also undertook an interview study with an explicitly personal intent.

I think that the most interesting aspect of the process related to my interaction with the 20 interviewees.... I conducted hour-long (at least) in-depth interviews with each of them. I tried to formalize–regularize this process as much as I could; however, I knew before I started that the more I would try to control the process, the less real wisdom I would get from the discussions. So the tension between doing "legitimate" qualitative research and getting the deepest possible responses from my interviewees became one the most interesting challenges that I confronted; ... I regularly strayed from my format as I became more and more willing to "participate" in the "participatory" method.

Katie describes some of the methodological connections to self.

I think because our doctoral program embraces the qualitative paradigm, there's a natural tendency to value the self and self-knowledge at least equally with the "body of knowledge" that has been generated by the "experts" out there. There really is an attention to integrating theory, practice, and self through reflection and dialogue.

Linda offers more detail in the following excerpt from her thesis:

<u>Deriving Criteria from Boyer's Characterization:</u>

Although it is not customary to develop the criteria for judging one's own dissertation, it seems to be a necessary step at this point. Boyer's four characteristics … are an excellent starting point for developing such criteria. This list I propose must be considered as a work in progress … (and as additional to recognized scholarly standards). [pp. 11–12]

METHODOLOGY—PARTICIPATORY RESEARCH

When it comes to uncovering intellectuals' underlying visions of their subjects, as well as determining their levels of passion toward them and the degree of their will to fight for their continuance, traditional social–scientific methods such as surveys will not work. I knew I needed to ask probing questions in personal interviews, where formal methods for generating quantitative "data collection" could easily be sacrificed in response to the richness and spontaneity of the intimate, unhurried conversational inquiry that permitted probes for additional clarification, examples, and so on.

Because I needed to know my interview subjects as "human beings," I realized that they would also have to know me on the same very human level. Thus, I would have to be an active participant in each of the conversations I was having. I made it clear during my initial contacts with each of my subjects that I was not just a researcher, I was also a strong advocate of "philosophy-as-integrative-practice." In some cases, such obvious interview bias could be a drawback, especially with interviewees who might see the interviewer as an authority figure. However, I knew that that would not be a problem in my case. The philosophers and integrative scholars I was interviewing were all well-established in their fields, and certainly did not view me as an authority figure. Thus I had no serious concerns that my "data" might be contaminated either by my spirited advocacy or my spontaneous, highly individualized reactions and questions....

Just as with the interviews, the summarization process itself is also participatory. Whatever accuracy I have achieved comes less from any attempts at traditionally uninvolved scientific objectivity as from my desire to see philosophy-as-integrative-practice survive somewhere in the academy. However, I don't mean to imply that I intend to use this personal participation as an excuse to maintain my own fixed notions on the subject. Many of my ideas and perceptions changed significantly as a result of conducting the interviews, and they are duly reflected in the results, which follow. [pp. 208–210]

Specifics of the Interview Methodology

One reason I chose to do in-depth and highly interactive interviews is because I knew that I would be dealing with words and concepts (e.g., "philosophy" and "integration") whose subtle meanings could not be captured or developed in questionnaires or other quantitative approaches. [p. 210]

Sharon also reflects on the intensely personal nature of her work: "To some extent, my ethnography is autobiographical, reflecting my own development of 'critical consciousness.'" Diana stated her perspective in chapter 6, if you wish to return to it now.

WRITING, PART TWO

Most correspondents find the interaction of writer and researcher—that is, the researcher as writer, methodologist as interpreter—as one of the complicating issues of their work. Paula writes:

One other decision rule I will address dealt with the case-reporting mode. I felt (instinctively knew?) that my dissertation should be reported in a "scientific mode" (whatever that means). I wrote in a factual, organized, journalistic, day-by-day chronicle, reporting only facts and for the most part omitting my feelings, thoughts, perceptions, and presumptions. I included my feelings, thoughts, perceptions, and presumptions in the summary of the case reports and in the final chapter of my dissertation. I wanted to report the cases in this way so that the reader could draw his or her own conclusions. When my major professor read the case reports, the suggestion in many instances was "Why haven't you commented on this?" Or she would write "you should comment on this." Most of the time, I had commented on these areas in the summary, case findings, or final chapter. I believed (and still do believe) that the case report should include only events that took place. Feelings, etc., of the reporter–researcher belong in a separate area.

Kathy shares her struggle with the "human" aspect of being a researcher–writer as she was experiencing it. "I am writing a case study and was led to believe that I should report my observations as objectively as possible. I resisted including my reactions and wasn't sure whether analysis and discussion should or could be a part of the narrative I was writing." Diana writes that "issues of voice and representation strike me as the most important and challenging aspects of my dissertation work." Ann expresses her predisposition prior to finishing: "Having spent some time, energy and enjoyment collecting interview data, I would like it to be reported richly and fully with limited academic cutback between what they say and I say. Such a style puts qualitative data in a supporting role and makes it rather dry."

One correspondent speaks more candidly:

> Regarding the methodology, there is a section on me as the researcher. I found this difficult to write because I am a very private person and because of my personal history. When having to compose that section, I felt "naked." Am I making sense? Judith, I am talking about the incident as an 8 year old, when I was told that I had to control my temper. I learned to control my temper, but in controlling my temper,

> I also learned to control all of my emotions, which is both good and not so good.... Was my research biased?.... I believe all research is, because each researcher brings his or her experiences, expectations, and judgments to the "laboratory" or "field."

Speaking of "academic cutback," in my original notes about the writing of this book I asked myself numerous questions, particularly after the first round of reviews suggested I needed to put more of "me" into it. The questions included: "Whose voice is this anyway?" "What is the purpose of any book? This book?" "What are the readers expecting? A meaning?" "How do you open up the possibilities for meanings rather than converge on "the" point?" In the first edition I wrote that "until qualitative researchers (who are writers?) are able to articulate the possibilities for reading within their texts and readers of qualitative studies are experienced in expecting possibilities, the former are going to have to provide some explicit guides to sensemaking." For this edition, there are more qualitative researchers who are able—and willing—to be vulnerable in their presentations and representations, to take risks in their writing, choice of topic, and so on.

The understandings and choices Paula and Ann articulated earlier reflect concerns that still exist; correspondents writing for the second edition recall different kinds of choices and decisions. From Chapter 3 of his thesis Chris writes:

> Cynthia Ozick (1991) writes that through metaphorical concentration we come to imagine the other, to imagine an existence—a perspective—different from our own. At the end of her essay titled "Metaphor and Memory," she writes:

>> Through metaphor, the past has the capacity to imagine us and we it. Through metaphorical concentration, doctors can imagine what it is to be their patients. Those who have no pain can imagine those who suffer. Those at the center can imagine what it is to be outside. The strong can imagine the weak. Illuminated lives can imagine the dark. Poets in their twilight can imagine the borders of stellar fire. We strangers can imagine the familiar hearts of strangers. (p. 283)

Metaphors inculcate experience with possibilities, with alternative visions our own perspectives could never account for if left only to feed on experience. Yet, as I tried to show in the previous chapter, metaphors are poor substitutes for experience. Metaphors offer us possibilities beyond experience but never in place of it, even as experience itself is interpreted in terms metaphoric.

Thus, speaking as an ethnographer and a teacher I offer this: that we, as ethnographers and educators, imagine ourselves, beyond all our pedagogical innovations and proclamations of standardized expectations, beyond our theory-driven, category-inspired understandings, as other than who we are—that we imagine ourselves as those we observe, teach, and interact with every day. Although this chapter is about research methodology in general and ethnography in particular, I cannot help but feel that what I say here applies equally to human interaction in many situations. In this chapter, I continue where I left off in chapter 2 and speak of the power of experience, both real and imagined, and of story, both fiction and nonfiction, in shaping one's consciousness and perspective of the world. While later chapters use my descriptions and interpretations of TeenStreet to define and honor the capacity of experience and story to nurture and enhance consciousness and perspective, this chapter established their limitations, or more specifically, the limitations of all human perspectives in relation to others. Such an understanding is a prerequisite for understanding the theory of human interaction I present in chapter 4. Thus, in this chapter I want to take a string, so to speak, and beginning with my understanding of both the type of ethnography I have tried to do and my and the TeenStreet teenagers' places within that ethnography, weave together what I understand of stories and how they illuminate possible existences while never fully giving away all possibilities. I present part of what I understand of TeenStreet, and what I understand of myself as an ethnographer, as an introduction to the concept of *imaginal inter-action* [italics added]. (pp.50–51)

Writing exercises were designed to allow stories to be shared and used by others in their own storytelling and to get the teenagers to look at their own lives. As part of the TeenStreet creative process, the exercises were conducive to *imaginal interaction* [italics added], or the creative interaction of words and actions as a way of imagining alternative perspectives by exploring one's own and others'. (p. 75)

Linda dove into her study; she describes one of the balancing acts of qualitative research and how the scales can "tip," particularly when one is interested and invested fully in the topic.

I do remember that I regularly strayed from my format as I became more and more willing to "participate" in the "participatory" method. Did I stray to the point that I no longer have a piece of legitimate qualitative research? I don't know and I really don't care. Can participatory research ever become too unstructured? As a holistic philosopher, my answer is "no." The truth is found in the raise of an eyebrow, the hesitation before an answer, the off-handed comment, the rich creative interaction in the moment. As I continued the participatory research, I realized that it was more like a living literature search—what a great opportunity it provided to ask questions of interesting thinkers before they died.

Linda continues: "The dissertation's methodology and arguments rolled into each other, sometimes to the point of confusion and at other times to a point of delicious wholeness."

Kelly shares one of her strategies that supported her ability to represent such "wholeness."

I guess here is as good a place as any to mention what I consider a unique aspect of my inquiry and write-up process.

In the course of interviewing the women, I made a conscious effort to solicit any images, metaphors, sounds or
other sensations that were related to the various aspects of
the experiences they were describing. Together, we explored the details and emotions connected to their mental
imagery and I probed for expressions of personal meaning
associated with these perceptions. These "data" along with
their narrative data helped me move closer to my goal of
developing as authentic a re-presentation of their expressions as I possibly could. Again, my underlying philosophy
for this approach is wide and deep.... This particular aspect
of my approach to inquiry resulted in my developing paintings that, like my 'write'-up, attempt to provide my readers–viewers with as broad and authentic a re-presentation
of what I understood as possible.

I wrote to Kelly and asked if there were really paintings in her thesis. The
answer is "YES!"

I am beginning to think the value of these letters, issues, and concerns is
that the correspondents are writing about decisions they made in order to
share, in written form, the "whole" as a meaningful context. Often the
whole includes enhanced self-understanding, given shared interests or
professions, shared background or heritage. What, then, is the research
"context" at this point, when we enter—in a sense—exploring ourselves?
In the past, the label would be "subjective" and "biased." My sense now is
a return to critical ethnography, a purposeful exploration from an insider's
perspective, a chance to make explicit and give voice to the unspoken, the
unheard, the invisible. We have traveled some mental miles since Elliot
Eisner's (April, 1993) Presidential Address to the American Educational
Research Association (AERA). What is meaning, who makes it when,
where, and how remain questions qualitative researchers willing to risk
complexity, confusion, difficulty, and multiple alternatives—as well as
deep understanding, rich description, and shared, silent assumptions—appear to be willing and able to make. "Meaning"—as being able
to be converged on by number or sentence; that is, a thing external to be
shared in some concise form to be underlined or abstracted and thus "ab-
sorbed" by an audience—is not the point of a qualitative research project
or any kind of "qualitative" experience.

QUESTIONS

1. What is your writing style? How will you express the inter-
    mingling of you, the researcher, with the context of your
    study? What choices or models are available to you? What
    is appropriate? Acceptable? Why?

2. Which choices or models do you prefer? Which can you
    defend? Does "paradigm" influence your decision here?
    Why or why not? Do any of the correspondents' styles
    "seem right" to you? Why?

3. What are your "goals" for the dissertation? Will articulat-
    ing what you expect from yourself support your decision
    making and refine your methodological approach and
    analyses?

4. What do you want to demonstrate with the completion of
    your thesis? Will or can your writing style facilitate your
    purposes? Who is your audience(s)? Will it matter?

Nancy's thesis, *A Rhetoric for Naturalistic Inquiry*, poses an argument
for ways to write up qualitative research:

> The most important section of my dissertation, I feel, is the
> demonstration chapter (Chapter V). It contains some writ-
> ing samples—e.g., illustrating scene-by-scene construc-
> tion, use of dialogue, and detailing of status life
> indicators—these are relatively harmless writing tech-
> niques. I also argue that the use of the third-person subjec-
> tive point of view takes the writer a step toward fiction and,
> while very effective (e.g., see Tom Wolfe's *The Right
> Stuff*), can leave the researcher open to criticism regarding
> trustworthiness. For the same reason, the interior mono-
> logue and creation of composite characters are not writing
> techniques that I would recommend for researchers, espe-
> cially doctoral candidates needing to please the limited
> readership of his/her committee.

Nancy's continued thinking, reading, and writing about writing since the completion of her thesis has also led her to revise some of her conclusions. She writes:

> Regarding Chapter VI of my thesis, "An Act of Discovery"—I've been thinking a lot lately about the inherent dangers of doing and writing qualitative research. To this end, I obtained a copy of the Judith Stacey article "Can There Be a Feminist Ethnography?" and have been editing the relevant section in Chapter VI of my dissertation ("Limitations of the Proposed Rhetoric for Naturalistic Inquiry").

Although the dissertation study will have an end point, the thinking and interacting with the thoughts and material the experience generates will probably not. Novice qualitative researchers want some help understanding what is possible and acceptable. As Kathy reflects, a finite conception about the processes of qualitative research would have been useful:

> Writing takes time. I still don't know how you determine the degree of detail to include in descriptions. I was asked that by one committee member. I tried writing a draft of a results or findings chapter and reacted to the feedback I got from the three people who read it. I would have welcomed information on writing the dissertation and the possibilities and options that exist. I know that those possibilities only exist if they are approved by the doctoral committee, but a chapter on the range of possibilities might help students and committee members as well.

Pam infers a good question in her most recent writing to me: "My intent is to work and focus on this like I have never done before from September to May 2000–2001; the absence of real deadlines contributes to the failure to produce." And Gretchen writes that she, too, desired some additional methodological support for doing qualitative research: "Developing a coding scheme, complete with rules for interpretation of categories, was something where I wished for more input from my committee, but none of them had much experience in this area."

For the qualitative researcher, "doing" research is synonymous with multiple simultaneous actions. Inaction also takes a variety of forms; ambiguous deadlines—either student or committee set—can hurt. The researcher as human instrument is a methodologist, analyst, writer, thinker, interpreter, inquirer—an individual human being capable of and responsible for some kind of final, organized presentation of the interaction of experience in context. Is it any wonder that chapters on analysis are difficult to compose? It's a lot of work. Paula recalls how she organized her writing:

> The organizational format I used included numbering each paragraph of the case reports (much like a legal document) and referencing these paragraphs when I discussed the case findings. This format aided me in two ways: (1) It helped me maintain an exemplary audit trail. I found the audit trail especially helpful during rewrites, when I omitted paragraphs and parts of paragraphs in an effort to improve the case reports; I didn't want the final case report to look like a data dump. (2) The reader could more readily see the reason for my finding statements. In other words, I documented my findings. It was worth the effort. BY NOW I GUESS YOU CAN SEE THAT I AM A VERY ORGANIZED PERSON! [NOTE: The concept of an audit trail (Halpern & Schwandt, 1986; Lincoln & Guba, 1985) supports the logical documentation of the evolution (not necessarily logical!) of the thesis.]

QUALITATIVE AND QUANTITATIVE

Concepts from scientific research remain prime target areas of concern for doctoral students in disciplines or institutions where qualitative research is not yet a norm. Students still write seeking support in target areas of "generalizability," "bias," and "validity," for example. Gretchen recalls:

> My committee was happy with my statement that field studies have limited generalizability.... Reviewers for journals such as the *NCA Quarterly*, *Communication Studies*, and *Human Communication Research* have been less kind; they have criticized my submitted articles for the lack of generalizability.

Kathryn remembers being concerned about this issue as well:

> In the methods chapter I devoted a good deal of paper to description of the sample and included more in the appendix. I described typical and atypical courses of illness. I included as much data as I thought would convey to doubters that these individuals were coping with serious illness; the "rich description" rule became very important because my sample was nonrandom.

I clearly stated my position on generalizability:

> The acute myocardial infarction (AMI) patients interviewed in this study seem representative of AMI patients in general and those described in other studies. However, extensive descriptive information is provided because the sampling method was nonrandom. These descriptive data may enable potential readers to examine the fit between this study sample and any other sample for which the findings might apply (Kirk and Miller, 1986; Le Compte and Goetz, 1982; Lincoln and Guba, 1985; Sandelowski, 1986). (pp. 35–36)

I addressed the issue of sample size as follows:

> The criteria more often identified for determining appropriate sample size in qualitative research is sampling to the point of redundancy or the point at which continued inquiry reveals no new data. Experience with the pilot study suggested a priori that a sample of 30 would assure encountering this redundancy phenomenon. (p. 36)

Jean raises another issue surrounding the sample—qualitative or quantitative. In the following excerpt, she shares her thinking around other methodological issues.

I had to go through the Human Subjects Review Panel at the University but did not have any problems, because the authors I studied had made appropriate legal arrangements with the collection about their works. I had to have letters from them and the collection bound within the pages of the dissertation. These letters were enough for the University, but University Microfilms had other ideas. I have just spent the last 3 months getting additional documentation to suit them.

She continues:

I believe that there is a tie or link between the way in which naturalistic inquiry is conducted and whether or not it is perceived as easy or rigorous.... If the structure is sloppy and the elements of a well-organized study are not present or poorly or improperly carried out, the study becomes suspect—even if the writing is of Pulitzer Prize quality. I look for elements such as the establishment of and continual work at trustworthiness; triangulation; how initial and continued entrance, confidentiality, and anonymity are handled; whether field journals are kept and their condition; whether an audit trail is maintained; whether a member check has been provided for and used; etc. I think if a researcher conducting naturalistic inquiry doesn't consider such elements, then the resulting research may be viewed with suspicion.

And she adds:

I believe that statistics, because they are one step back from people who create or generate them, are somehow viewed as "cleansed" and free of bias. Statistics, by their very nature and definition, have been stripped of context and appear somehow "cleaner." (The woman from the Graduate School at my college may be "getting by" at her university because her study is statistical in nature. The subjects of her study might be viewed as numbers and not people.)

Mishler (1986) cites Cicourel ("Interviews, Surveys, and the Problems of Ecological Validity" in *American Sociologist*, 17) when he asks, "'Do our instruments capture the daily life conditions, opinions, values, attitudes, and knowledge base of those we study as expressed in their natural habitat?'" (p. 24). Mishler and Cicourel are discussing issues surrounding research interviewing, but I believe that question should be addressed by every researcher and asked of every study.

QUESTIONS

5. Have you looked at any dissertations for examples of style? Have you read any of the current literature dealing with the writing of qualitative research, or read research articles describing or exemplifying it? Is the writing as important as the substance, results, hypotheses, and interpretations? Why or why not?

6. Which, if any, writing techniques are expected in your dissertation document? Which reference format? Are voice and tense already mandated? How will you find out?

7. Are you familiar with audit trail techniques? Computer sorting and coding packages? Are you a "detail" person? If not, can anything discussed in this book so far support your qualitative research efforts? If so, what are the "logical" choices for you? Why?

8. Do you know the major research journals in your field? Have you examined their contents over the past 5 years for trends and exemplars? Where are things changing? What seems to remain the same? Will either of these last two questions influence the final presentation of your material? Your choice of focus and methodology? Why or why not? Can you afford to be—are you expected to be—"cutting edge" with your thesis?

9. What do you know about the Human Subjects Review Panel at your university?

10. What do you need to know about the Graduate School's requirements for ANYTHING related to the appearance and substance of your thesis? What other questions might you ask of someone there?

11. What do all these thoughts on writing have to do with methods and analysis? Has reading the excerpts from the correspondents enabled you to see how some qualitative researchers made sense of things? Do any of their strategies make explicit to you the kinds of thinking and decision making that is a part of analysis?

12. Does reading these letters help you to begin to shape your own sense of direction, give voice to your own needs and concerns, and highlight where you are already A-OK?

13. How rigorous is your study? By whose standards? What models? Which examples?

14. Do you have some understanding of the ramifications of your decision making around writing, methodological, and analysis issues? For example, is generalizability an issue for you? Will you change? Will journals? What are the tradeoffs? What is important?

DATA COLLECTION AND ANALYSIS

Several correspondents, including Ann in the following excerpt, comment on the technical aspects of data collection:

> The ideal method would have been to videotape, but there was no way to do so without intruding on the process I was examining; also due to confidentiality concerns, permission would not have been given for videotaping. Even with audiotape, some participants were reluctant to participate.

This was planned as a multimethod study: content analysis of tape recordings, coding of double interacts, observation of the communication process (including nonverbal communication), and follow-up interviews.

Pat describes how her study evolved and was recorded:

The chairperson of my committee and the department head permitted the study to move forward "over time." My study involved analyzing kindergarten block play throughout the school year. Videotape was accumulated at the beginning, middle, and end of the school year. No interviewing was done of the participants, but informal discussions were undertaken with parents to determine where the different subjects came from which appeared in the dramatic play. The committee's concern was if I could get permission from the school district and if I would manage the technical gathering of the data.

The analysis reflected my understanding of children and what I "saw" on the videotape. The themes and categories I "named" truly emerged from the videotape and required the "grouping" of like aspects into the category. I am proud to say that no tables appear in my dissertation. To support the selected categories, I used direct quotations from the episodes, which are a sequential reporting of the taped block play. (I developed a typology of block play and drew from 6 episodes the extent of block play found in this group. No two episodes used the same format; however, there was demonstrated consistency in some aspects of block play across episodes.)

Robert remembers his committee's concern with his chosen methodological framework:

I found that my chosen methodologies bore the most scrutiny from my committee. They appeared satisfied with the research design once I convinced them of its rigor. The appendix of my dissertation is loaded with evidence showing interview questions and responses; the number of times each question was asked; observed teaching (using a Hunter-based observation tool); principal behavior; and other data to provide detailed information about the school and the community. Tapes, written logs, and journals have been retained in my files. This detailed collection helped to silence the question, how much is enough?

Robert also describes his sampling procedure:

Selecting the school to be studied required the use of quantitative data. Some committee members objected to using two test results, so I incorporated questionnaires (sent to area school administrators, teachers, and IU directors) requesting their impressions of the schools under consideration for the study. I also used a state survey to elicit teachers' opinions of their own school. The thoroughness of the selection process satisfied the committee.

Ann's reflections remain critical of the distance from text to experience:

As I am doing my research, I have a better idea of my analytical process. I have found Bogdan and Biklen's (1982) analysis chapter very helpful and reassuring if I start worrying again about the "right" answer and choosing themes and categories. They suggest "follow some sensible organization"; the themes and questions of my questionnaire are proving to be very helpful categories. Also, I'm very glad I spent a good deal of time thinking about what exactly I wanted to find out and organized quite a structured interview, although I resisted this at first.

At first glimpse, it might appear that Ann has a totally a priori focus, which is incompatible with qualitative research. You may recall, however, that Ann undertook a pilot study from which her focus became clearer in her own mind. At a certain point, qualitative researchers must determine what they are and are not doing. During the interaction of method and analysis, converging on a focus and making subsequent decisions to support that choice appears to be a common sensemaking strategy. Jane found that returning to the texts while engaged in field research is helpful. She writes:

> It has been very useful to go back to various methods books now, as I work on data analysis. Although I had read them before, tidbits are much more meaningful now that I'm into it. I guess that's true of any learning: It's meaningful when applied to a context. The advice and examples in methods books are reassuring and sometimes provide direction. Lincoln and Guba's (1985) *Naturalistic Inquiry* has been more helpful to me now than previously, when I was just learning about the methods. I really appreciate their humor, e.g., the first 90% of the project takes 90% of the time; the last 10% takes the other 90%.
>
> I had thought I would be farther along by now; evidently that's typical of such studies. But then again, I experience that emotional roller coaster and sometimes think, "I am in good shape! It's really moving now!"
>
> I was frustrated earlier this summer because I thought I could whip out the introduction, methods, and literature review chapters, but I found I couldn't complete them until I had gotten into data analysis. Now I realize for me that's appropriate and OK. Because I've done some analysis, my focus is clearer and that will improve those preliminary chapters.

Susan also found that the literature review is not a "once-and-for-all" chapter.

> The literature that I had started with for my proposal framed my questions initially. It wasn't until after I had interviewed my first three groups of students that I really changed my focus to the resulting study. The literature was general enough about transfer students and time-to-degree

that the questions were broad and open-ended. It was easy to use the questions I began with to interview the remainder of the students. After I finished all the interviews with all the participants, I added to the literature review.

Carol describes her experience with "analysis" a little differently.

> I interviewed my participants, taped all of the interviews, transcribed them, and then mailed the transcripts back to those interviewed to have them check for content and meaning. Then I sat and look at the transcripts for a long time. It was a hot summer in 1988! Eventually, I was able to identify some common themes. These were described as "emerging themes."… At the end of analyzing the transcripts and identifying the emerging themes, I invited those interviewed to meet with me and review them together. About half of them responded. This provided another check on my perceptions.

Susan did not undertake a member check:

> One thing I did not do was to member check completely. I felt that my time frame was too short to risk sending chapters to administrators for their input. I made sure that they knew what I heard during the interviews, I was careful to get clarification, and I was careful to get my facts straight about the policy. There has been only one participant who offered any comments. She questioned a quote I attributed to her. I know she said it, she doesn't remember saying it. It certainly wasn't inflammatory or in any way did it cast a bad light on her, she just doesn't remember saying it. If I had it to do over again and I had more time I certainly would have sent chapters to participants for review.

Jean, even after finishing, can't quite put her finger on how things came together for her, a feeling reminiscent of some of Helen's comments at the conclusion of chapter 7.

Are you familiar with Louise Rosenblatt's (1978) <u>The Reader, the Text, the Poem</u> in which she argues for the transactional view of language? Her work certainly influenced my study. I am not sure how the themes emerged. I looked for what appeared to be common themes within both writers and their papers. The writing process as defined and discussed by Graves, Smith, Calkins, Murray, and others has between three and four "stages." I used a variation on those stages in examining the papers, so I had a structure. I also knew that I wanted to look at the writers' lives as well as their works, so that also added to the structure.

Susan also addresses "structure," reiterating the reality that initial forms will almost undoubtedly give way as analysis occurs.

After I had gotten all the information I could about the mandated measures, the opinions of the administrators, and the time-to-degree related info from the students, I had to come up with a theoretical framework. The framework <u>did not</u> frame my interviews. In fact, I had started with a totally different framework and soon discovered that it simply wouldn't work with the information that I had. Constant comparison (sound familiar?) helped me see that I had something that was related, but what? It was during a coffee break with a friend that we visualized the current framework.

The question of rigor is concomitant with chapters on methodology and analysis. The books listed in chapter 5 address methodological and analysis issues such as trustworthiness, dependability, and "validity." As of this writing, thinkers and practitioners of qualitative research have made some strong statements in regard to these issues, but questions remain. (See back issues of the *Educational Researcher,* or Eisner & Peshkin (1990) *Qualitative Inquiry in Education: The Continuing Debate* and Guba (1990) *The Paradigm Dialog.*) I do think the correspondents are implicitly and explicitly stressing the importance of understanding the methodological choices doctoral students and their committees make. Acquiring a solid background in qualitative research methodologies can only support your decision making.

QUESTIONS

15. Analysis is still difficult to articulate explicitly. How much ambiguity are you willing to live with? Do you trust your own abilities to think, relate, connect, resift, reconsider, change? How much support will you require from your committee? From others?

16. What ethical issues are embedded in all that has been shared so far? How much time do you have for seeking permissions, working with drafts, providing feedback, and getting feedback?

17. What does being the research instrument mean? Can you separate "you" from the context? Why or why not? What are the implications of your choices?

18. Are any of the correspondents' suggestions useful? What sense of the qualities of the qualitative are you deriving?

SUMMARY

It is a predestined conclusion; understanding may only come about by doing. Books and practice inform and enrich each other. Novice qualitative researchers seem to depend on their experience, the texts, and other people as they gain confidence in grasping the complexity of the task. As many who have written me report, sharing experiences with others is a source of simultaneous commiseration and strength, because, as Edwina writes, "it's" not always easy: "Another frustration I had was the inability to get the information I needed—questionnaires were misinterpreted or not completed, people were unavailable, writing impossible to read."

Commitment and dedication are also required in collaborative projects. Although more than several correspondents wrote about their work with their respondents, Kim explicitly described her thesis as "collaborative and arts-based":

The research was part of a $85,000 grant funded by Apple
Computers, Inc. Margaret Fitzgerald, the elementary music teacher I collaborated with, and I were frustrated on
how to adapt for special needs children in the music classroom. I focused on learning disabled children.... Margaret
was interested in ADHD [attention deficit and hyperactiv-
ity disorder] kids and if they would be able to focus better
using the computer or learning in a traditional music classroom....

There is a chapter in the book *Music Makes the Difference*
(MENC [Music Educators National Conference], 1999) that
Margaret and I wrote about our project. The book is about
collaborative relationships in music education. The project
was awarded the Computerworld/Smithsonian Innovations
in Technology Award last year. Materials on our project are
part of the permanent collection of the Smithsonian.

At some point, novice qualitative researchers must share what they are
doing with their committee; several correspondents wrote about the interaction with their committees during the data collection and analysis phase
of their studies; frustrations are expressed here, too.

It would have helped if I or my major professor would have
clarified the relationship that should exist between me and
the committee members while collecting and analyzing
data and while writing the study. I assumed it was up to me
and my major professor to plod along. We met regularly. I
gave other committee members a draft of the first four
chapters and received feedback immediately from one of
the four. I never knew how actively or persistently I should
seek their feedback. They all were so busy.

When the second committee member responded with comments almost 3 months later, I felt that I was being asked to
reevaluate my data, my questions, and the way I had been
working during that time period. It appears that these rela-

tionships differ from place to place and among departments. My goal is to finish Draft 1 this weekend and
revisions next weekend. I will respond about defending
this masterpiece when I am finished with that phase.
Thanks for caring about us. This is an incredible learning
process. I did not anticipate the emotional reactions that often are linked to exhaustion and being a 44-year-old
woman. Everything seems to take longer than anticipated. I
finally gave up estimating and started pushing harder....
Enough for now. I am returning to chapter 9. Pulling it all
together is difficult, too. I have discovered so many interesting questions in the process of looking closely. I am convinced that qualitative studies are worth doing. I am not
sure I believe the traditional dissertation format, our rite of
passage to the community of scholars, is necessary. I probably would have benefited just as much from writing a report to the coordinators of the project I studied and two
articles either collaboratively with them or with input from
the participants I studied. Perhaps I am just tired and looking for an easier way out.

Another correspondent reflects:

I have no evidence that anyone on the committee fully read
my dissertation until about 3 weeks before I defended. My
advisor was away for the summer and though I sent him
chapters weekly, as we had agreed, he never sent them back
and never commented on them until he returned. Probably
he had read them and thought they were okay. I couldn't
tell. He never communicated with me. (It's a good thing I
was fairly confident.) When he got back into town, he read
the whole thing and said it was fine, that it was time to stop
writing.

Just as we are individuals, so too, then, will the questions, concerns, decisions, and outcomes of our studies reflect our individual educations and
interactions. Providing support for making wise choices based on a solid

understanding of qualitative research methodologies is what all the books I've seen on qualitative research are attempting to do. Mary concludes: "It's very cathartic to type and read my thoughts about what's happening to me during this doctoral process. I see a variety of levels of progress during the past 5 years." So, too, will you.

9

UNDERSTANDING BY FINISHING

Defining "The End"

One thing that I would highly recommend to your readers is that they be incredibly detailed in their research. Duh. I thought I was. I read and re-read my study, silently and out loud, and still, still I made a mistake. I am somewhat embarrassed to admit this but when I quoted my now boss in my study, three different times in three different places, I got her title wrong—in three different ways! It wasn't until after it was all bound and finished, and I gave her a copy to read for her comments that the blunder was discovered—by her, not me. Oh my gosh! She still hired me and fortunately has a good sense of humor. Yikes! (Susan)

Defining the end is not easy, as we are never in an absolute sense quite there. Although most of the correspondents expressed relief at being finished, several chose to write in some detail about bringing closure to the dissertation experience. Edwina writes: "The major frustration, however, was that once I completed the study, defended the dissertation, and graduated, that was the end of it. The results of years of work and sweat stand on a dusty shelf in a library somewhere, having no effects on future teachers of writing. I had hoped to prove so much."

PUBLICATION

If I am understanding the ramifications of the following correspondent's thoughts, perhaps publication concerns need to be addressed much earlier in the research process, perhaps even prior to methods and focus. The question of audience, which was addressed in the earlier chapters of this book, reappears in more detail.

> The dissertation has yielded several convention papers but so far no publications. The articles including no quantitative tables have been rejected outright from the scholarly journals in my field. Those which have focused on the last minute, a priori hypotheses have rated "revise and submit" letters. I am still in the process of reworking and resubmitting or sending to other journals.

> I am presently an assistant professor in my 3rd year. If I am to be considered for tenure, I need to have a minimum of 6 or 7 research articles published in high quality academic journals. At times I find myself wishing I had chosen a quantitative project for my dissertation. Although editorial policies state an interest in both quantitative and qualitative studies, they do not yet accept many qualitative studies in my field.

> I have hopes of publishing two chapters from my dissertation as separate books.... I have presented some of my data in the form of a paper ... which will be published in the proceedings' volume. I have written a couple of pieces as a result of that effort. They are "making the rounds." Perhaps because one of the participants in my study is somewhat controversial (which was one of the reasons I was drawn to this person), a couple of the major journals in the field have been reluctant to consider the articles.

As I began work for this second edition, I attempted to contact all of the correspondents from the first edition; several responded, many did not. I suspect Jean Stevenson and several others are published by now. Indeed, Marie Nelson and Stuart Sigman were already authors when the first edition hit the press; Nancy Zeller and Maria Piantanida have published since.

Kathy poses some questions relevant to the writing of the dissertation. They reflect some of the concerns highlighted in earlier chapters, specifically, for whom is the dissertation being written?

All of the dissertations I read followed the five chapter quantitative format. This is different from the style and format developing in the reports of qualitative studies in journal articles and books.

Should the models be changing as we continue to explore possibilities? I read recently that many dissertations are being written using the style and format of manuscripts and articles that can be submitted for publication. Is this happening in colleges of education? Or do the rules regarding form and style we impose on dissertations create documents for our committee members and other doctoral students looking for models or possibilities? I have a hunch that the continuing efforts doctoral students choosing to use qualitative research for their theses make will have a major impact on the "rules regarding form and style." As a doctoral student, you are in a unique position of learning and understanding. You may be working alone or with your peers and committee. Most importantly, perhaps, you are actively engaged in seeking answers to your questions about theory and practice. Reflecting and writing about those questions can direct you and others toward possible answers.

Almost 9 months after the 1991 Qualitative Research in Education conference, Kathy sent me a brief letter highlighting dissertation experiences she found most memorable. As I read the letter, I thought it brought a sense of closure to the experience of doing thesis research in general and qualitative research in specific. The following paragraphs might have as easily been written as bullets and titled "Tips for the Qualitative Researcher"; they could easily have introduced this book as well.

Dear Judy,

The enclosed notes were written in July when I was cleaning out files; I had scribbled on the pad that you might be interested in having them? Here goes.

Pay attention to responses you give when people ask what your dissertation is about. Every response refines and clarifies the important findings and relationships.

I found that I drew diagrams and illustrations on a pad when I met with my advisor but I failed to date these scribbled illustrations. These were important steps in formulating an organizational schema but I didn't realize it.

Regular conferences with your major professor, coresearchers, etc. are important. I've read that regular conferences are important for analytic and psychological security. I agree.

I wish I would have dated articles I copied and read along the way. I would recommend dating everything and keeping a notebook handy at all times.

Driving provides an opportunity for thinking and analyzing categories, relationships, etc. Metaphors seem to come to mind while driving places, or running. The danger is that one's head becomes so occupied with thoughts and possibilities that traffic violations are common among doctoral students—speeding, running stop signs, failing to renew drivers' licenses. I was surprised to learn that I was not alone when I began to compare occurrences with others.

I also cried a lot during the year I was working on my dissertation. I blamed it on being 40-something, but I learned that fellow graduate students in their 20s and 30s cried a lot. I was at a meeting one day when I was overtired and started crying when asked to do a small task. People apologized for things that had not offended me. I just couldn't envision one more thing to do on top of the dissertation deadlines that I felt I couldn't meet. Everything seems to take longer than I anticipated.

There needs to be a stopping point. Analysis and refining diagrams can go on indefinitely and there is so much data, so many interesting tidbits to explore in this type of study.

Preparing to defend a qualitative study requires simplifying findings and presenting highlights. Expect the unexpected. The questions asked and comments made validate the importance of qualitative studies. Committee members react to different occurrences and details. The readers take away what is pertinent to them.

I was disappointed that I didn't get enough feedback from committee members during my defense. I didn't realize that the defense also marked the end of the doctoral program and my relationship with people I respected. I wanted more from them than the structure of the defense allowed. I wasn't sure what my role during the defense should be. Could I have redirected questions or asked questions of committee members or was my role solely to respond, to explain and clarify?

It is over! I graduated and the copies are being bound. I became a better writer in the process and continuously appreciated the complexity of human interactions and of schooling. The word dilemma took on new meaning. Dilemmas were a part of my life.

Sincerely, Kathy Rojek

Kathy's letter portrays, perhaps, a traditional way to image "the end." We look back on our experience and recall the peaks and valleys. Another perspective on "the end" requires one to conceptualize the entire process of doing a qualitative dissertation as enabling an individual to get "there"; imagining the hurdles of ambiguity can enable the novice qualitative researcher to adjust his or her stride. The questions, concerns and issues that are answered, solved, or avoided become pieces of the final whole.

Few correspondents even mentioned their final defense; Katie is one who did: "I'm not sure exactly what I did have to defend, other than the degree to which I honored the methods I'd learned about and used, and the degree to which participants told me that what I wrote about is what they meant." But as one correspondent relates in the following story, all the aphorisms about finishing (e.g., it's not over 'til it's over) need to be carefully heeded. Defending the end is not the same as finishing.

AFTER THE DEFENSE

The Politics of the Graduate School

My story begins only after the defense had taken place. My committee signed off on the dissertation and I was left—alone, literally—to negotiate the dissertation's acceptance with the Graduate School. The excitement of the completion of the defense was rudely tempered with the problems the Graduate School presented. It was as if I entered a "different game" with new players or rules with no support or assistance from my committee or the School of Education. I did not know that the "General" existed within the Graduate School who would manipulate me further. I thought the "war" had been won once the defense had been completed. I was to learn a "new" lesson.

My department had had only one qualitative dissertation go through the Graduate School (only five dissertations in all) less than 8 weeks before mine, and it had been difficult. My co-chair advised me to use a "particular" typist to complete the job. I had initially resisted the suggestion thinking I could do it myself. (I viewed myself as able to type, use the computer, and spell check, and knowledgeable enough of the required style format to accept the corrections which might come from the reader; money, of course, was a major concern.)

I came to understand why using "this" typist was so important as the final drafts of chapters were reworked. I became unable to see the need for corrections and the revisions were very slow to complete. I had worked with the copy so long that I was unable to read what was written and often would read what I thought was there on the page.

My typist was an individual who knew the style format and the Graduate School staff like the back of her hand. She had served as a typist for many others within the University complex and was well respected. She worked in a medical lab and was very good at cleaning up and clearing up jargon that made the text less than clear while knowing and appreciating different dissertation formats. She enjoyed the type of dissertation I presented to her. She not only typed the text but also edited the final product.

This typist told me repeatedly how helpful I was with what I brought to her, and how easy the job would be to complete. She often told me not to worry. It must have been obvious how nervous I was, as once again I felt "powerless" because I had to rely on others for assistance in the completion of the dissertation.

I found myself renegotiating my dissertation with the Graduate School staff acting as the final decision maker. This Graduate School staff was a single decision maker, a secretary, who followed the traditional five chapter format approach. Having my typist, however, gave me "insider" status, because she was seen as "one of their own." I had only to mention her name and possible questions or problems seemed to be manageable. When I turned in the first draft, I was asked to supply the name of the typist. When I gave her name, I was reassured that there would probably be no problem.

My first problem had to do with the transcripts of my data that my committee had required me to include as an appendix. My committee had felt it was important for others to have access to the transcripts from which my categories came. The presentation was not initially acceptable to the Graduate School, i.e., the secretary. For example: The Graduate School did not like the printer I used for my data (transcripts). They wanted the entire transcription of my data to be retyped to be consistent with the remainder of the document. My typist said it was not necessary as it was "raw data." The style manual does not call for "raw data" to be presented in such a format since they were to appear as an appendix. (I did not check this fact. My typist's matter-of-fact response led to a telephone exchange with the Graduate School. Mary commanded enough power within the Graduate School to let this aspect of my appendices be reported as they originally appeared ... saving me some money, which was my typist's point in "calling the secretary's hand.")

I finished in August, the very busiest time for the Graduate School. The outside person selected to read my dissertation was only used in cases when everyone else was busy. This reader did not understand her job; she edited the format I chose, which was different from the standard five chapter design, by making remarks that indicated to me she did not understand qualitative research. There was no problem with the references, grammar, or spelling, but over and over in the document she used her green pen to remark: "WHY IS THIS HERE AGAIN? I'VE READ THIS BEFORE?" Receiving the manuscript for corrections, I could not believe that page after page would have something circled or crossed out that had nothing to do with grammar, spelling, or citation reference. I was furious! I took the "box" (containing the dissertation) back to my typist, who was as upset as I was. She told me that this reader was not often used, and she would make a call to the Graduate School. (It cost me another $50.00 to recover the material which had been marred by her green pen. This did not include the transcript appendix in which the reader continued to question, marking with green pen.) ...

My final run-in with the Graduate School involved the page numbering, which was out of sequence by the end of all this. The office had looked over the dissertation four times and had not caught it. At this late date, they were asking me to rework the dissertation because I had two pages numbered 104. I refused. I asked to speak to the Dean. I was denied personal or phone access. He told the Graduate School to "take care of it." My point was simply after four proofs it was not my problem. Page numbering had never been identified as a "needed correction." The secretary gave up and numbered the pages 104 and 104b.

From all these experiences occurring during an 8-week period, I have learned that using the techniques of qualitative research to complete the dissertation process are helpful. My typist was an "informant." I would probably still be negotiating with the Graduate School if she had not been part of my "team." (It must be mentioned that my committee all went on vacation after my defense. I hope no one else has a story sequence like mine. I learned so much about "the system" completing my dissertation, it's a wonder I want to work in higher education!)

It has taken me several sittings at the computer to write this to you. Although it has been nearly 9 months since these events occurred, I still get upset reliving them. Maybe someone else could benefit from the story of the typist who could walk the mine field.

Defining the end is something a qualitative researcher is only in the position to do at the end (rather than at a proposal hearing, chapter checkpoints, etc.), when it is finally able to be constructed from the interaction of the researcher with context. Some of our methodologies, strategies, and perhaps even contexts may compare across researches. But the interactions of person with context; researcher with researched; human being with him- or herself and among others; individual as writer, analyzer, and interpreter are multiple, integrated, and often simultaneous; they are human and "of" us as individuals. They can be made explicit and shared.

Perhaps that is why I am not so sure that the previous story and Kathy's letter shouldn't be the first chapter of this book. Although we are accustomed to begin at the beginning, defining the possibilities and problems of endings might help us better prepare for the trip ahead, which is the idea with which this book began. It is not a new idea; I think Aesop probably had it in mind a long time ago, as have most of our grandparents and even ourselves—that is, we can and do learn from the experiences of others, even as we commit to charging ahead into our own. Although we consider the author of the story to be crucial in getting "the" point(s) across, what we the readers and listeners choose to learn from the described experience is up to us.

Learning with and through others is a fundamental quality of the qualitative. The level of analysis of "war stories" is not purely the acceptance or rejection of thick description; the description can, for example, provide insights into possible interpretations of action or examples of experiences to either seek out or avoid. It can simply increase the awareness of the possibilities within a particular context. Through them, a novice inquirer and faculty or family member can grasp the ambiguities of context and process inherent in the pursuit of the doctorate by means of qualitative research. In addition, those of us committed to pushing our understandings of the qualities of the qualitative can use such commentaries to provoke our thinking on issues critical to responsible and humane research.

10

UNDERSTANDING BY ENDING

Beginning With Endings

> As I look back, it strikes me that my writing has evolved over time ...; my doctoral experience marked a time when I became more of a connected knower and writer.... I think it's a lot about finding voice and becoming more confident about what I think and say and write about—and feeling supported in that process. (Katie)

Reviewers for the second edition encouraged me to put more of "me" in this book. I remain convinced that there is plenty of me here, even before I made so many explicit comments and connecting statements. Is qualitative research about the researcher, who defines the needle, spins the thread, and pieces together the understandings; or is it about the "context," richly defined? Does the audience for this text want to know about me—or have they found situations to avoid and ideas to try as a result of becoming a part of a community of individuals who have undertaken—and therefore understand and have some insight into—the processes the novice is now going through? Have they found support? Only with such fine and patient correspondents could I have provided this opportunity. In this same chapter of the first edition, I wrote:

> I have a diagram in my notes; there is a line = arrow = the researcher directed toward a bull's eye = target = context. The perspective from the tip of the arrow prior to entering the field (the arrow lined up to the target from 100 yards away) looks differently than the target from the tip of the arrow immersed in the context. At some point, the arrow is removed from or falls out of the context, and again, the per-

spective from the tip changes. As Joseph Heller's book title suggests, *Something Happened.* Qualitative researchers leave their mark not only in the context but also on any resulting documentation and discussions. Not only are they learning about a particular context, but they are also learning from and with it. Meaning is mobile, transitory and cumulative. (Meloy, 1994, p. 85)

Meaning is also the result of energy, emotion, and time expended.

How do I conclude this second edition? What has it meant to me? What I have I learned from my correspondents and from my reflection and writing to and for you? My first commitments remain:

- I still mean this book to be supportive in ways I cannot be to people whom I may never meet. There are emerging cohorts of individuals who support each other's and the neophyte's attempts at doing qualitative research. I wrote this book in hopes of being a part of these efforts.

- I also mean this book to provoke questions; I have heard others ask many of the ones written herein. I think sharing some answers—or the possibilities of better questions—is useful. I mean to expose, rather than resolve, issues, concerns, and problems that face doctoral students, their families, and committee members.

- I mean this book to be a contribution, not to determining "the" meaning of thinking about and doing qualitative research for one's thesis, but to the thinking about and doing of qualitative research in general.

As I traced the issues running throughout the pages of this book, I noted the following themes in the first edition:

- limited opportunities for some graduate students to learn about qualitative research and the limitations of some learning;

- the complexity and ambiguity surrounding the multiple, simultaneous processes of doing qualitative research and of being the research instrument;

- qualitative researchers are decision makers and sense makers; they are—or become—writers;

- the implicit and explicit power relationships surrounding the formulating, doing, and reporting of qualitative research for the dissertation;

- learning occurs by reading, doing, talking, thinking, sharing, feeling, writing, reflecting;

- qualitative dissertations and research appear to represent attempts at expressing a "whole" of experience.

I have also commented on the following themes in this second edition:

- the explicit autobiographical nature of qualitative research;

- the emotional aspects of learning and doing;

- ethics and the novice researcher;

- the continued need for clear thinking and strong background knowledge;

- qualitative research is an adventure that takes patience, focus, courage, heart, and support;

- issues of positionality, technology, representation, and presentation have only begun to be hinted at herein.

I cannot say in "conclusion," because I am probably at yet another beginning, laden with some thoughts that had not occurred until the organizing, writing, and editing of this book. "How-to" books will tell us what to do and which rules to follow. Experience will guide us in minute ways that the books have not yet made clear. Colleagues, peers, and colearners will push the levels of understanding in order to clarify possible meanings—for future researchers <u>and</u> researches. But mostly, the candid reflections of 40 individuals who have lived many aspects of your journey will keep you company when you feel alone. They will help you anticipate and plan ahead for the success of your qualitative dissertation. At this juncture, it makes sense to offer the second letter promised in chapter 1, in order to provide an articulate, uninterrupted example of the qualitative research endeavor. Dr. Wolar's eloquent letter and "excellent adventure" provide the promise of the possible:

My doctoral dissertation was researched within the discipline of history. My specialty, if you will, concerned the American West. Ultimately, my dissertation pertained to 20th century environmental–landscape issues pervading the American West.

I desperately desired to do something novel ... to do "cutting edge" research ... to actually attempt to do original research ... to stand out from the crowd of dissertations. That crowd is particularly focused upon issues of ethnicity, race, gender, and class, and I found those issues to be intellectually stale and boring. I can recall my dissertation advisor telling me to try to choose a research topic in which I was personally engaged on some level. Why? Because I would be involved in that topic for many years ... well beyond the actual years involved in the research and writing of the dissertation. In effect, he was advising me that my dissertation would be a part of the remainder of my life. He also mentioned that, if possible, I should try to research something that would involve some travel in the West. We are both interested in the visual images of the West, so it was an excellent piece of advice.

For several years prior to the research experience, I had mentally toyed with the idea of researching the concept of trails in the 20th century West. After all, much of America's 19th century experience in the West revolved around various trail systems. Seemingly, the concept of trail had died in the 20th century with the advent of the automobile, railroads, and airplanes. In fact, trails were being used in a specifically recreational capacity—within the remaining wildernesses of the nation. An avid mountaineer, I wondered whether our capacity to utilize recreational wilderness trails in the 20th century said something deeper about the American character. So, I asked a simple question: Where, and when, did Americans first construct recreational wilderness trails in the American West? What did such construction reflect in the way of cultural, philosophical, spiritual–religious, and landscape-engineering values? After running the idea by my dissertation advisor, I was told that I had the "green light" to proceed. Both of us acknowledged that it appeared to be an area of Western research never before attempted; and, possibly for good reasons: a paucity of primary source materials and a general lack of intellectual creativity to frame appropriate historical questions.

Bottom line? I was in uncharted historical research seas. There was no model for me to study beforehand, no prior research that was directly relevant to my proposed topic. In essence, I was to be the research model in this endeavor. That realization was simultaneously unnerving and exciting. I needed to have faith in myself and my intellectual hunches, the courage to relentlessly pursue the evidence (if any existed), and the tenacity to go on the "firing line" in defense of those research interests. Organization of the dissertation, without any previous model in my hands, proved to be a very challenging task.

I immersed myself in wilderness reading, outdoor recreational reading, exploratory journals from the 19th century, and histories of the Forest Service and the National Park Service. This background material led me to formulate a series of substantive questions that I posed to myself. I shared those questions with my dissertation advisor, who declared that I appeared to be asking qualitatively important historical questions. We agreed that, since I was financing my own research (realistically, my university was unable to be of any viable financial assistance in this endeavor), I would take approximately 3–4 months to do preliminary research. If, at the end of that time period, nothing in the way of relevant primary source materials surfaced, I would abandon the topical concept and move toward a list of alternative research projects.

After exhausting what I thought might be relevant secondary source materials, and after doing an exploratory search
on the Internet, I decided to dip into possible primary
source materials at a prestigious archival institution: The
Huntington Library (San Marino, CA). Serendipity struck.
I happened on a small archive relating to the origins of the
Pacific Crest Trail [PCT], a recreational wilderness trail
stretching from the Canadian–Washington border to the
California–Mexico border. Apparently, nobody was aware
of this material. I was on my way.

Shortly thereafter, upon doing an additional web site
search, serendipity struck again. I happened on a name that
appeared to coincide with a name that I remembered seeing
in those PCT papers at the Huntington Library. I wrote the
folks on the web site a letter and inquired as to whether my
hunches might be correct. I hit the Mother Lode. I had effectively "discovered" a rather large archive pertaining to
the origins of the Pacific Crest Trail. It dwarfed the materials previously found at the Huntington Library. I think it
would be no exaggeration to state that this archive was
thousands of times larger than that which I perused at the
Huntington Library. I was, to say the least, quite excited by
this discovery ... in the garage of a family residence.

But, would this be a dissertation about the Pacific Crest
Trail exclusively? No, that would be too narrow ... although it could have been the focus of a very viable research project on its own terms. I would craft a hefty
dissertation chapter out of my new discovery, and allow the
evidence within those archival materials to launch me into
several peripheral relevant directions.

The research pace quickened after my "discovery." Now I
had confirmation that my trails project was viable and original. It would superficially be a research project about the
establishment of recreational wilderness trails in the Amer-

ican West. On a deeper level, it would be a novel attempt at explaining the American intellectual transition toward wilderness preservation and away from wilderness aggrandizement. Also, and most importantly, it would be (literally and figuratively) a research project that emanated from the ground up: The concept of trail was about to be the platform for intellectual musings on wilderness, American industrial mechanization, philosophical–spiritual–religious accommodations to such modernization, landscape engineering, and the development of a subtle shift in consciousness within American society. It would not be an environmental history, per se, but a landscape history (a small subdiscipline within the general arena of environmental history) that attempted to chart something that is exceedingly difficult for historians: the consciousness of a people.

The title seemed to tell all: "The Conceptualization and Development of Pedestrian Recreational Wilderness Trails in the American West, 1890–1940: A Landscape History." I researched not only at the Huntington Library, but at the Bancroft Library in Berkeley, CA; the following national parks: Glacier, Yosemite, Sequoia–Kings Canyon, and Rocky Mountain; the James J. Hill Reference Library in St. Paul, MN; various historical societies in California and Minnesota; the John Muir Papers in Stockton, CA; and the Denver Public Library. I made use of papers from the Appalachian Trail Conference, the Boy Scouts of America, the Mountaineers (Seattle), the Sierra Club, and others. It was a gratifying, humbling, and fulfilling experience.

In the midst of the research and writing, I became an informal agent on behalf of the "discovered" archival papers. I arranged a meeting between the familial custodians of the papers and the Huntington Library. Recently, the Huntington Library has informed me that they have formally acquired the collection for posterity. I am thrilled.

If I was unable to physically review particular papers, I was able to arrange mailed copies of such via e-mail communications. E-mail became a particularly valuable tool with regard to appropriate research contacts. My dissertation advisor is a very prominent historian of the American West, and I can candidly admit that using his name opened a few research doors quickly. My dissertation advisor allowed me the maximum intellectual freedom in pursuing my topically and conceptually original research. He did not require any revisions that reflected his personal desires concerning that which should, or should not, be included within the dissertation. He did not require the submission of separate chapters for review. He simply wanted me to turn in the first draft of a finished product. If I had questions, he answered them and served as an encouragement to continue my research.

The actual research took approximately 1 year and 9 months of full-time work (January, 1996, to September 7, 1997). I began writing on September 7, 1997, and concluded writing on March 17, 1998. I did nothing but write full-time. All research travel was done by automobile, and I wrote the dissertation at four locations. Changing the writing scenery was particularly vital and effective in keeping my creative energy charged. I had read a study wherein it was stated that the single most important habit in concluding the Ph.D. dissertation was to never cease working on it. Therefore, it was important to write every day, even if only a small portion was completed on a given day. I succeeded in writing every single day for 6 months; and fortunately, never fought "writer's block" in any way. I was very inspired by the exercise of accumulating my massive evidence, developing a plan of organization, and writing in disciplined fashion. I averaged just under 100 pages per month, or just over 3 pages of text per day. The final product, including 32 pages of bibliography, was 582 pages. Ironically, the most difficult portion of the writing pertained to the acknowledgments page and the required abstract page.

The defense of the dissertation went quite smoothly. Fortunately, only very minor editorial revisions were necessary after submission of the first draft to my dissertation advisor. As I recall, my dissertation advisor reviewed the finished first draft in April, 1998, returned it with written comments (as well as verbal), and the full four-person dissertation committee reviewed it in June or July. Conflicting summer schedules precluded a defense until September, 1998. I graduated in December, 1998. Fortunately, as well, the graduate school found nearly no grammatical errors on proofreading the final product.

Unlike so many dissertation writers, I found the experience to be one of the most sublimely rewarding experiences of my life. I actually noted regret as I realized that I was close to finishing the product. It was a once-in-a-lifetime experience that is unlikely to be duplicated.

My advice to the doctoral student is as follows: Listen to your dissertation advisor; display vision and courage in formulating a research project; do not rush the project for the sake of finishing the program; do not write until reasonably assured that your research is complete; and write every day, in disciplined fashion, once you have decided to commence writing.

Wow. Here's to hope, adventure, success, and challenge! To close, again, for the last time, I will end where I began, with thoughts from Marilyn.

Blatantly autobiographical or not, dissertations are "about" selves who write; S explained to me that in doing her master's thesis she learned to do research; in doing her dissertation, to write. B confirms this: People often speak of having learned to write while writing their dissertations. On the one hand, what an odd thing to say. Haven't we all been students long enough to have learned, already, how to write? One oughtn't scale—either up or down—a precipice without proper gear and training. But on the other hand, one has to say "of course"; this learning is the nature of initiation rituals—in writing the dissertation one learns a complex "writing" of discipline and identity. One might almost capitalize the "W." Having learned already to write, then, what Writing am I expected to learn in writing the dissertation—what *discipline* and *identity*? [italics added]

Perhaps the answer to Marilyn's question is the discipline required of a knowing, learning identity, sometimes referred to as "a qualitative researcher" ... that is, YOU!

APPENDIX A

About the Research Correspondents

- Lew Allen, EdD (1992). *Shared Governance: A Case Study of a Primary School.* University of Georgia.

- Anonymous

- Ann, a doctoral student. ["Ann" is a pseudonym. I am grateful to be able to use her letters. Per her request, I have removed any significant references to place or topic.]

- Carol, EdD (1989). [Although I had early permission from "Carol" to use her material, we have lost contact. Therefore, I have chosen to use some of the material with "Carol" as the attached pseudonym.]

- Dana Haight Cattani, PhD (1998). *Broad Authority: Young Women and Teaching.* Stanford University. Research interests: sociology of education, teacher education and induction. E-mail: dana_cattani@stanfordalumni.org

- Mary K. Clark, PhD (1999). *Determinants of Overall Satisfaction of a Summer Transition Program at the University of Michigan.* Research interests: equity in graduate education, retention and transition programs. E-mail: mkclark@umich.edu

- Pamela K. Edwards, PhD, in progress, Iowa State University. Research interests: learning over the life span, balancing adult lives, the power of stories. E-mail: drscdwards@home.com

- Robert M. Foster, EdD (1988). *One Good School: A Study of an Effective Elementary School Using Ethnographic Research Methods.* Lehigh University.

- Katharine S. Furney, EdD (1997). *Caring as the Cornerstone of Change: A Cross-Case Analysis of Three Schools' Experiences in Implementing General and Special Education Reform.* University of Vermont. Research interests: policy implementation, women and leadership, collaborative teaching at the university level. E-mail: kfurney@zoo.uvm.edu

- Pat M. Garlikov, PhD (1990). *Block Play in Kindergarten: A Naturalistic Study.* University of Alabama–Birmingham.

- Diana L. Haleman, EdD (1998). *"That's Not Who I Am": Contested Definitions of Single Motherhood.* University of Kentucky. Research interests: social justice issues; rural schools, women's issues.

- Linda S. Handelman, PhD (1995). *The Knowledge Fragmentation Crisis in Higher Education: Can Philosophy Help?* Claremont Graduate University. Research interests: philosophy as citizen education. E-mail: lshandel@yahoo.com

- Lisa A. Haston, doctoral student, Michigan State University. Expected graduation date: Summer 2001. Research interests: academic advising, adult learners, community colleges. E-mail: hastonli@msu.edu

- Kelly Clark Keefe, EdD (1999). *Moving Beyond Recognition: Voices of Women Academics That Have Experience Being First-Generation College Students.* University of Vermont. Research interests: sociocultural influcences on educational experiences, gender, arts-based social science research. E-mail: kaclark@zoo.uvm.edu

- Patricia Kovel-Jarboe, PhD (1986). *An Analysis of Organizational Culture During Change.* University of Minnesota.

- Sharon Shockley Lee, EdD (1992). *Hegemony in an Elementary School: The Principal as Organic Intellectual.* University of Missouri, St. Louis. Research interests: principal and teacher preparation; professional development schools; ethics, equity, and social justice in education. E-mail: shalee@siue.edu

- Timothy McCollum, Masters student, University of Georgia.

- Kimberly A. McCord, DME (1999). *Music Composition Using Music Technology by Elementary Children With Learning Disabilities: An Exploratory Case Study.* University of Northern Colorado. Research interests: music and special education, music technology, jazz education. E-mail: KIMBERL678@aol.com

- Sally Michlin, PhD (2000). *Pedagogy for Undergraduate, Lower Level, English Courses: The Application of Educational Psychology and Learning Theories to Teaching Literature and Rhetorical Writing.* Kennedy-Western University, Cheyenne, Wyoming. Research interests: adult education, methodology, social dynamics. E-mail: michlins@sacredheart.edu

- Marie Wilson Nelson, EdD (1982). *Writers Who Teach: A Naturalistic Investigation.* University of Georgia.

- Kristin Park, PhD (1992). *To Aid the Stranger in our Midst: Sacrifice, Religiosity, and Gratitude in Three Sanctuary Churches.* University of North Carolina, Chapel Hill.

- Jane F. Patton, EdD (1991). *A Case Study of a Community College's Program of Cultural Pluralism.* University of Southern California.

- Paula Gastenveld Payne, EdD (1990). *Power Communication Skills in Three Female College Presidents: A Descriptive Study.* Vanderbilt University.

- Maria Piantanida, PhD (1982). *The Practice of Hospital Education: A Grounded Theory Study.* University of Pittsburgh.

- Susan L. Poch, PhD (1998). *Accountability in Washington's Public Higher Education Institutions: Do Community College Transfer Students Fit In?* Washington State University. Research interests: transfer students, policies, and issues; family science. E-mail: poch@wsu.edu

- Gretchen S. Rauschenberg, PhD (1986). *Reducing Equivocality and Assembling Summaries: A Weickian Analysis of the Information Organizing Processes of a North Central Association On-Site Evaluation Team.* Ohio University.

- Barbara Smith Reddish, EdD (1999). *A Postmodern Analysis of the Little Red Riding Hood Tale.* University of Massachusetts. Research interests: reading recovery, literacy acquisition, multicultural children's literature. E-mail: reddishb@polaris.umpi.maine.edu

- Kathy Rojek, EdD (1991). *Teachers as Decision Makers in a District-Wide Project.* University of Georgia.

- Helen Rolfe, PhD (1990). *Case Studies of the Implementation of an Instructional Change in Two Elementary Schools.* University of Virginia.

- Edwina Portelle Romero, PhD (1999). *Strange Bedfellows: Integrating Form and Content in Teaching Composition.* University of New Mexico, Albuquerque. Research interests: writing, writing theory, feminism, pedagogy. E-mail eromero@lvti.cc.nm.us

- Janice Ross, PhD (1998). *The Feminization of Physical Culture: The Beginnings of Dance in American Higher Education.* Stanford University. Research interests: arts and cognition, dance education. E-mail: JROSS@leland.stanford.edu

- Kathryn A. Scherck, DNSc (1989). *Coping With Acute Myocardial Infarction.* Rush University.

- Stuart J. Sigman, PhD (1982). *Some Communicational Aspects of Patient Placement and Careers in Two Nursing Homes.* University of Pennsylvania.

- James Sullivan, EdD (1992). *Long Island Secondary Assistant Principals: A Study of Role Perceptions, Responsibilities, Frustrations, and Satisfactions.* Hofstra. Research interests: High school climate/culture, leadership. E-mail: VAN55@ix.netcom.com

- Jean M. Stevenson, PhD (1989). *The Writing Processes of Theodore Taylor and Jane Yolen.* University of North Dakota.

- Marilyn Volger Urion, PhD (1998). *Becoming Most Fully Ourselves: Gender, Voice, and Ritual in Dissertations.* Michigan Technological University, Houghton, MI. Research interests: student decision making regarding graduate school persistence. E-mail: mjurion@mtu.edu

- Ellen Weber, PhD (1994). *A Multiple Intelligence View of Learning at the High School Level.* University of British Columbia. Research interests: secondary and higher education renewal. E-mail: eweber@houghton.edu

- Glynn G. Wolar, PhD (1998). *The Conceptualization and Development of Pedestrian Recreational Trails in the American West, 1890–1945: A Landscape History.* Research interests: wilderness consciousness, "space and place" landscape consciousness in the American West, intellectual history.

- Christopher M. Worthman, PhD (1999). *Different Eyes: Imagery, Interaction, and Literacy Development at TeenStreet.* University of Illinois at Chicago. Research interests: community-based literacy practices, critical literacy. E-mail: cworthma@wppost.depaul.edu

- Nancy Zeller, PhD (1987). *A Rhetoric for Naturalistic Inquiry.* Indiana University, Bloomington.

APPENDIX B

Sample Tables of Contents

EXAMPLE 1

*Accountability in Washington's Public Higher Education
Institutions: Do Community College Transfer Students Fit In?*

Susan Poch, 1998, Washington State University

TABLE OF CONTENTS

EXECUTIVE SUMMARY

LIST OF TABLES

LIST OF FIGURES

CHAPTER

1. INTRODUCTION
   The Study
   Purpose of the Study
   Significance of the Study
   Limitations of the Study
   Overview of the Study

EXAMPLE 2

*Some Communicational Aspects of Patient Placement
and Careers in Two Nursing Homes*

Stuart Jay Sigman, University of Pennsylvania, 1982

TABLE OF CONTENTS

PREFACE

CHAPTER

EXAMPLE 3

*"That's Not Who I Am": Contested Definitions of
Single Motherhood.*

Diana L. Haleman, University of Kentucky,
Lexington, 1998

TABLE OF CONTENTS

Annie

Rebecca

Chelsea

Jean Ella

Elaine

Gloria

Dawnita

Frankie

Hannah

Irene

APPENDIX C

Barbara's Letter, Continued

12/7/98

Dear Judy,

Where do I begin? I am flattered by your prompt and lengthy response, intrigued by your use of pencil, amused by your town's name (is it Poultry?), and delighted to be engaged in this conversation. My 10-year-old son has gone to bed at 7:00 PM (!) leaving me with unexpected free time, and I can't resist responding to your letter. Do not hesitate to "interrupt the flow with questions" as your good questions help me to formulate my thoughts. You see, I chose to be a part of this discussion quite deliberately as I feel that it will help me to define my research lens. I learn by processing, or talking through my problems—"thinking out loud" if you will. Right now I am learning various research paradigms and struggling to define my own personal perspective. My hope is that this discussion will assist in that process, making this a mutually beneficial experience, and closely connected with my work....

You ask, "What has become of the strange vocabulary and the secret society?" Well, the initial barriers seem to have diminished somewhat. As I continue to speak about research with professors, or other doctoral students, the language gradually becomes familiar—I guess I am being immersed in the culture much like I would if I traveled to a foreign country. I think that my particular study, that of gender depictions in children's literature, has certainly been instrumental in my being able to find a comfort level with research—because it is meaningful to me, in very personal ways, but is simultaneously scholarly and intellectually alive, which holds my interest. The methodology, literary criticism, is an integral part of what is meaningful, i.e., I thoroughly enjoy deconstructing the essay—analyzing every component under the microscope (the lens of which I haven't yet defined). *To interview people and transcribe conversations, or to observe people and take field notes would be overwhelming to me, I think. I would be unable to stop, unable to contain it. I would continue to ask deeper questions to want to know more, to analyze further and to make connections to everything, whereas a book is already self-contained. There is a finite amount of information for me to scrutinize.*

I should note that this writing is wholly unrehearsed, and these thoughts are as new to me as they will be to the reader. I am thinking out loud as I write, and realizing these thoughts for the first time. This is a great "Aha" for me, this notion that live subjects would over-whelm me, whereas books sit on shelves until I am able to deal with them—at my convenience. So ... human subjects would be uncomfort-able for two reasons; there would be the conflict between not wanting to distance myself (subject and "other") and ultimately becoming overly involved, and the frustration of having to negotiate logistical accommodations with living, breathing, thinking beings versus still, silent books who sit patiently waiting for me. [italics added]

Anyway, your next question concerns how I perceive myself as a learner, researcher, "member of a secret society." My gut response is that I feel proud of having accomplished this level of scholarship, but an altogether interesting phenomenon occurs in the process. The higher the academic level I reach (we could measure this in de-grees—ha ha) the more humble I feel. I understand that intelligence is relative, and that there are many kinds of intelligence (á la Howard Gardner) and that academic achievement does not necessarily equate to what I consider to be intelligence. Intelligence, for me, is being a whole person; thinking and acting rationally, being kind, being toler-ant, and listening a lot. It is *not* being able to speak academically ex-clusive language. Coincidentally, as I learn this language, I am less likely to actually use it unless there are no other words that express my thoughts adequately. I do, however, strive to find the perfect adjective and encourage my students to expand their vocabularies, but this is different from using academically exclusive language—this is merely being articulate. As for being a LEARNER—I am a life-long one. This is perhaps an overused term (life-long LEARNER) which unfor-tunately serves to undermine its meaning, but I know very well that I will continue to learn for as long as I am able, through reading, through listening, and through teaching.

[I left off here, last time. It's about a week later, and I have some more free time]

I've reread your letter, and you've asked my thoughts on moving beyond feminism. The authors who have influenced me in this thinking are the postmortem poststructuralist feminists such as Judith Butler, Ann Garry, Marilyn Pearsall, bell hooks, Allison Weir, Alison Assiter. Feminist literary critique is just too restrictive for me.... Anyway, my ultimate lens will be an eclectic one, I'm sure....

I guess I'll end here, and wait for your next "prompt." Feel free to ask about any aspect of the research, as I enjoy writing about it, as the writing helps me to understand what I'm doing. Take care.

Barbara Smith Reddish

BIBLIOGRAPHY

Aisenberg, N., & Harrington, M. (1988).*Women of academe: Outsiders in the sacred grove.* Amherst: University of Massachusetts Press.

Bamberger, J. (1991). *The mind behind the musical ear: How children develop musical intelligence.* Cambridge, MA: Harvard University Press.

Barone, T. (1992a). Beyond theory and method: A case of critical storytelling. *Theory into Practice, XXXI (2),* 142–146.

Barone, T. (1992b). On the demise of subjectivity in educational inquiry. *Curriculum Inquiry, 22* (1), 25–38.

Barone, T. (1993). Breaking the mold: The new American student as strong poet. *Theory into Practice,* XXXII.

Bloom, L. R. (1998). *Under the sign of hope: Feminist methodology and narrative interpretation.* Albany, NY: State University of New York Press.

Bloom, L. R. (1999). Interpreting interpretations: Gender, sexuality and the practice *of not reading straight. Qualitative Studies in Education, 12* (4), 331–345.

Bogdan, R., & Biklen, S. (1982). *Qualitative research for education: An introduction to theory and methods.* Needham Heights, MA: Allyn and Bacon.

Brearly, L. (2000, June). *Exploring the creative voice in an academic context: Representations of the experience of transition.* Presentation at the twelfth annual conference of Ethnographic and Qualitative Research in Education, State University of New York, Albany, New York.

Bresler, L. (1996). Basic and applied qualitative research in music education. *Research Studies in Music Education, 6,* 5–15.

Brodkey, L. (1987a). Writing ethnographical narratives. *Written Communications, 4,* 25–50.

Brodkey, L. (1987b). Writing critical ethnographical narratives. *Anthropology & Education Quarterly, 18,* 67–77.

Buber, M. (1958, 1987). *I and thou.* New York: Collier Books.

Calkins, L. (1983). *Lessons from a child: On the teaching and learning of writing.* Portsmouth, NH: Heinemann Press.

Carini, P. F. (1979). *The art of seeing and the visibility of the person.* Grand Forks, ND: North Dakota Study Group on Evaluation.

Carter, K. (1993). The place of story in the study of teaching and teacher education. *Educational Researcher, 22* (1), 5–12.

Clandinin, D. J., & Connelly, F. M. (1996). Teacher professional knowledge landscapes: Teacher stories–stories of teacher–school stories–stories of schools. *Educational Researcher,* 25 (3), 24–30.

Cole, A., & Knowles, J. G. (2000, June*). Arts informed perspectives on qualitative research.* Presentation at the twelfth annual conference of Ethnographic and Qualitative Research in Education, State University of New York, Albany, New York.

Colwell, R. (1992). (Ed.). *Handbook of research on music teaching and learning.* New York: Schirmer Books.

Creswell, J. W. (1998*). Qualitative inquiry and research design: Choosing among five traditions.* Thousand Oaks, CA: Sage.

Cruz, C. (2000, June). *Feminist and post structural thoughts in educational research.* Presentation at the twelfth annual conference of Ethnographic and Qualitative Research in Education, State University of New York, Albany, New York.

DeCastell, S., & Walker, T. (1991). Identity, metamorphosis, and ethnographic research: What kind of story is "Ways with Words?" *Anthropology and Education Quarterly, 22,* 3–22.

Denzin, N. K., & Lincoln, Y. S. (Eds.). (1994, 1999). *Handbook of qualitative research.* Thousand Oaks, CA: Sage.

Delgado, R. (1996). *The coming race war?* NY: NYU Press.

DeLorenzo, L. C. (1987). An exploratory study of sixth–grade students' creative music problem solving processes in the general music class. *Dissertation Abstracts International.* 48(07),1689A. (University Microfilms No. 87–21099).

Duckworth, E. (1987). *'The Having of Wonderful Ideas' and Other Essays on Teaching and Learning.* New York: Teachers College Press.

Duncan, G. (1996). Space, place and the problematic of race: Black adolescent discourse as mediated action. *Journal of Negro Education, 65,* 133–150.

Eisner, E. W. (1991). *The Enlightened Eye.* New York: Macmillan.

Eisner, E. W. (1993). Forms of understanding and the future of educational research. *Educational Researcher, 22* (7), 5–11.

Eisner, E. W. (1997). The new frontier of qualitative research methodology. *Qualitative Inquiry, 3* (3), 259–273.

Eisner, E. W., & Peshkin, A. (Eds.). (1990). *Qualitative inquiry in education: The continuing debate.* New York: Teachers College Press.

Ellison, R. (1947, 1990). *Invisible man.* New York: Vintage.

Ely, M. (1991*). Doing qualitative research: Circles within circles.* London: Falmer Press.

Etter–Lewis, G. (1993). *My soul is my own: Oral narratives of African American women in the professions.* New York: Routledge.

Freeman, M. (2000). *Co–constructing meaning of the home–school partnership through narrative encounters.* Presentation at the twelfth annual conference of Ethnographic and Qualitative Research in Education, State University of New York, Albany, New York.

Glaser, B. G., & Strauss, L. (1967). *The discovery of grounded theory.* New York: Aldine de Gruyter.

Glesne, C. (1999). *Becoming qualitative researchers: An introduction.* Reading, MA: Addison Wesley.

Glesne, C., & Peshkin, A. (1992). *Becoming qualitative researchers: An introduction.* New York: Longman.

Goetz, J. P., & LeCompte, M. D. (1984). *Ethnography and qualitative design in educational research*. Orlando: Academic Press.

Greene, M. (1992). The passion of pluralism: Multiculturalism and the expanding community. *Journal of Negro Education, 61,* 250–261.

Greene, M. (1995). *Releasing the imagination: Essays on education, the arts, and social change.* San Francisco: Jossey–Bass.

Guba, E. G. (Ed.). (1990). *The Paradigm Dialog.* Newbury Park, CA: Sage.

Guba, E. G., & Lincoln, Y. S. (1981). *Effective Evaluation.* San Francisco: Jossey–Bass.

Guba, E. G., & Lincoln, Y. S. (1989). *Fourth generation evaluation.* Newbury Park, CA: Sage.

Halpern, E., & Schwandt, T. (1988). *Linking auditing and metaevaluation: Enhancing quality in applied research.* Newbury Park, CA: Sage.

Hamilton, R. (1993). On the way to the professoriate: The dissertation. *New Directions in Teaching and Learning, 54,* 47–56.

Heath, S. B. (1983). *Ways with words: Language, life, and work in communities and classrooms.* New York: Cambridge University Press.

Heller, C. (1997*). Until we are strong together: Women writers in the Tenderloin.* New York: Teachers College Press.

Heller, J. (1974). *Something happened.* New York: Knopf.

Hickey, M. (1995). *Qualitative and quantitative relationships between children's creative musical thinking processes and products.* (Unpublished doctoral dissertation, Northwestern University, Chicago.)

Holstoi, O. R. (1968). *Content analysis for the social sciences.* Reading, MA: Addison–Wesley.

Ives, E. D. (1980). *The tape–recorded interview: A manual for field workers in folklore and oral history.* University of Tennessee Press: Knoxville.

Kleinman, S., & Copp, M. A. (1993). *Emotions and fieldwork.* Newbury Park, CA: Sage.

Larson, C. (1992). *Self-representation in biographical and autobiographical narrative: Disclosing the assumptions of the inquirer.* Paper presented at the annual conference of the American Educational Research Association. San Francisco, California.

Lather, P. A. (1991). *Getting smart: Feminist research and pedagogy with/in the postmodern.* New York: Routledge.

LeCompte, M. D., & Goetz, J. P. (1982). Problems of reliability in ethnographic research. *Review of Educational Research, 52,* 31–60.

Levi, R. (1991). *A field investigation of the composing processes used by second grade children creating original language and music pieces.* Unpublished doctoral dissertation, Case Western Reserve University.

Lincoln, Y. S., & Guba, E. G. (1985). *Naturalistic inquiry.* Beverly Hills: Sage.

Mann, C., & Stewart, F. (2000). *Internet communication and qualitative research: A handbook for researching online.* Thousand Oaks, CA: Sage.

Marshall, C., & Rossman, G. (1989, 1995). *Designing qualitative research.* Beverly Hills, CA: Sage.

Meloy, J. M. (1986). *Organizational sensemaking: A study from the inside out.* Unpublished doctoral dissertation, Indiana University, Bloomington.

Meloy, J. M. (1989). Got a problem? In J. B. Allen & J. P. Goetz (Eds.), *Teaching and Learning Qualitative Traditions.* Athens, GA: The College of Education, The University of Georgia.

Meloy, J. M. (1992). *Writing the qualitative dissertation: Voices of experience.* Paper presented at the annual conference of the American Educational Research Association. San Francisco, California.

Meloy, J. M. (1993). Problems of writing and representation in qualitative inquiry. *Qualitative Studies in Education, 6* (4), 315–330.

Meloy, J. M. (1995). To be or not to be: Transcending a fact vs. fiction dichotomy. *Electronic Proceedings, The Qualitative Research in Education Conference.* Athens, GA: The College of Education, The University of Georgia.

Merriam, S. B. (1991, 1998). *Case study research in education: A qualitative approach.* San Francisco: Jossey–Bass.

Merryfield, M. (1992). *Constructing scenes and dialogues to display findings in case study reporting.* Paper presented at the annual conference of Qualitative Research in Education. Athens, Georgia.

Merchant, B. M., & Willis, A. I. (2001). *Multiple and intersecting identities in qualitative research.* Mahwah, NJ: Lawrence Erlbaum Associates.

Mishler, E. G. (1986). *Research interviewing: Context and narrative.* Cambridge, MA: Harvard University Press.

Mitchell, C. J. (1983) Case and situational analysis. *Sociological Review, 31* (2), 187–211.

Morgan, G. (1983). *Beyond method.* Beverly Hills: Sage.

Morson, G. S. (1996). *Narrative and freedom: The shadow of time.* New Haven, CT: Yale University Press.

Nelson, M. (1991). *At the point of need: Teaching basic and ESL writers.* Portsmouth, NH: Boynton/Cook.

Neuman, I., & Benz, R. R. (1998). *Qualitative-quantitative research methodology: exploring the interactive continuum.* Carbondale, IL: Southern Illinois University Press.

Ozick, C. (1989). *Metaphor & memory: Essays.* New York: Knopf, distributed by Random House.

Patton, M. Q. (1990). *Qualitative evaluation and research methods.* Beverly Hills: Sage.

Pike, K. (1967). *Language in relation to a unified theory of the structure of human behavior.* The Hague: Mouton.

Piper, T. R., Gentile, M., & Parks, S. D. (1993). *Can ethics be taught? Perspectives, challenges, and approaches at the Harvard Business School.* Boston, MA: Harvard Business School.

Probyn, E. (1993). *Sexing the self: Gendered positions in cultural studies.* London/New York: Routledge.

Rawls, J. (1971). *A theory of justice.* Cambridge, MA: Belknap Press of Harvard University Press.

Richardson, L. (1990). *Writing strategies.* Newbury Park, CA: Sage.

Rosenblatt, L. (1978). *The reader, the text, the poem.* Carbondale: Southern Illinois University Press.

Schatzman L. & Strauss A. L. (1973). *Field research: Strategies for a natural sociology.* Englewood Cliffs, NJ: Prentice Hall.

Seidman, I. (1991, 1998). *Interviewing as qualitative research: A guide for researchers in education and the social sciences.* New York: Teachers College Press.

Smith, J. K. (1988, March). The Evaluator/Researcher as Person vs. the Person as Evaluator/Researcher. *Educational Researcher*, 18–23.

Smith, J. K. (1992). *The stories educational researchers tell about themselves.* Paper presented at the annual conference of the American Educational Research Association. San Francisco, April.

Spradley, J. P. (1980). *Participant observation.* NewYork: Holt, Rinehart & Winston.

Stanage, S. (1987). *Adult education and phenomenological research: New directions for theory, practice and research.* Malabar, FL: R.E. Krieger.

Sternberg, D. (1981). *How to complete and survive a doctoral dissertation.* New York: St. Martin's Press.

Stewart, J. P., & Brizuela, B. M. (2000). Symposium: "Habits of thought and work" – The disciplines and qualitative research. *Harvard Educational Review, 70* (1), 22–108.

Taylor, S. J., & Bogdan, R. (1984). *Introduction to qualitative research methods.* New York: Wiley.

Taylor, V., & Bonham, A. (1992). *Gaining access to bureaucratic organizations.* Workshop presented at the annual conference on Qualitative Research in Education. University of Georgia, Athens.

Tillich, P. (1957*). Dynamics of faith.* New York: Harper.

Van Maanen, J. (1988). *Tales of the field: On writing ethnography.* Chicago, IL: University of Chicago Press.

Van Maanen, J. (1995). *Representation in ethnography.* Thousand Oaks, CA: Sage.

Weick, K. (1979). *The social psychology of organizing* (2nd ed.). New York: Random House.

Weick, K. (1995). *Sensemaking in organizations.* Thousand Oaks, CA: Sage.

Weis, L., & Fine, M. (2000). *Speed bumps: A student-friendly guide to qualitative research.* New York: Teachers College Press.

Weir, A. (1996). *Sacrificial logics: Feminist theory and the critique of identity.* New York: Routledge.

Wiggins, J. H. (1992). *The nature of children's musical learning in the context of a music classroom.* Unpublished doctoral dissertation, University of Illinois at Urbana–Champaign.

Wolcott, H. (1990). *Writing up qualitative research.* Newbury Park, CA: Sage.

Wolcott, H. (1995). *Transforming qualitative data: Description, analysis, and interpretation.* Thousand Oaks, CA: Sage.

Yin, R. K. (1984, 1994). *Case study research: Design and methods.* Newbury Park, CA: Sage.

Zeller, N., & Farmer, F. (1999). "Catchy, clever titles are not acceptable": Style, APA, and qualitative reporting. *Qualitative Studies in Education, 12* (1), 3–19.

Zwicky, J. (1992). *Lyric philosophy.* Toronto Studies In Philosophy. Toronto: U of Toronto Press.

AUTHOR INDEX

SUBJECT INDEX

(Author's note: Except for the correspondents' names, this index is but one version of how to make sense of this material.)